MONTGOMERY COLLEGE LIBRARY
GERMANTOWN CAMPUS

Generational Change in American Politics

Generational Change in American Politics

Paul R. Abramson
Michigan State University

Lexington Books
D.C. Heath and Company
Lexington, Massachusetts
Toronto   London

Library of Congress Cataloging in Publication Data

Abramson, Paul R.
  Generational change in American politics.

  Bibliography: p.
  Includes index.
  1. United States—Politics and government—1945- . 2. Voting—United States. 3. Young adults—United States—Political activity. I. Title.
  JK271.A27   324'.2'0973   74-27752
  ISBN 0-669-97741-1

Copyright © 1975 by D.C. Heath and Company.

All rights reserved. No part of this publication may be reproduced or transmitted in any form or by any means, electronic or mechanical, including photocopy, recording, or any information storage or retrieval system, without permission in writing from the publisher.

Published simultaneously in Canada.

Printed in the United States of America.

International Standard Book Number: 0-669-97741-1

Library of Congress Catalog Card Number: 74-27752

To Janet, Lee, and Heather

Contents

	List of Figures	ix
	List of Tables	xi
	Preface	xv
Chapter 1	**Forming the New Deal Coalition**	1
	The Depression and the Emergence of Class Voting	4
	Blacks and the New Deal Coalition	8
Chapter 2	**The Decline of Class-Based Politics in Postwar America**	11
	Economic and Social Changes in Postwar America	11
	Class Voting in Postwar Presidential Elections	13
	The Changing Social Composition of the Democratic Presidential Coalition	23
Chapter 3	**Generational Change and the Erosion of Class Voting**	29
	Age-Group Differences in Postwar Presidential Elections	30
	Partisan Change Among the Middle Class	42
	Generational Change and the Social Composition of the Democratic Presidential Coalition	46
Chapter 4	**Generational Change and the Decline of Party Identification**	51

	The Decline of Party Identification Among the White Electorate	52
	Age and Party Identification in the Mid-1950s	53
	Age and Party Identification Between 1952 and 1972	56
	Party Identification Among Blacks	65
	Concluding Comments	67
Chapter 5	**Towards a New Coalition?**	71
	Attitudes Among Age Cohorts in 1970 and 1972	74
	Feelings Toward Social Groups Among Age Cohorts in 1970 and 1972	84
Chapter 6	**Attitudes, Feelings, and Partisanship**	99
	Attitudes, Feelings, and Voting Behavior in 1972	100
	Attitudes, Feelings, and Party Identification in 1970 and 1972	109
Chapter 7	**Conclusions**	123
	Bibliography	127
	Index	135
	About the Author	141

List of Figures

2-1	Proportion of White Major-Party Voters Who Voted Democratic for President from 1944 through 1972, by Social Class	23
3-1	Proportion of White Major-Party Voters Who Voted for Truman in 1948, by Social Class and Age	31
3-2	Proportion of White Major-Party Voters Who Voted for Stevenson in 1952, by Social Class and Age	31
3-3	Proportion of White Major-Party Voters Who Voted for Stevenson in 1956, by Social Class and Age	32
3-4	Proportion of White Major-Party Voters Who Voted for Kennedy in 1960, by Social Class and Age	32
3-5	Proportion of White Major-Party Voters Who Voted for Johnson in 1964, by Social Class and Age	33
3-6	Proportion of White Major-Party Voters Who Voted for Humphrey in 1968, by Social Class and Age	33
3-7	Proportion of White Major-Party Voters Who Voted for McGovern in 1972, by Social Class and Age	34
5-1	"Feeling" Thermometer	85

List of Tables

1-1	Percentage of Adults Who Voted for Each Major Candidate Between 1920 and 1972	5
1-2	How Voted for President in 1944, by Social Class and Race	8
2-1	How Voted for President Between 1948 and 1972, by Social Class and Race	15
2-2	Percentage of White Major-Party Voters Who Voted Democratic, by Occupational Level	18
2-3	Social Composition of the Democratic Presidential Coalition from 1948 to 1972	24
3-1	Class Voting Among Whites, by Years of Birth in Seven Presidential Elections	35
3-2	Status Polarization Among Whites, by Years of Birth in Seven Presidential Elections	36
3-3	Social Composition of the Democratic Presidential Coalition from 1952 to 1972, by Years of Birth	47
4-1	Party Identification Among Whites from 1952 Through 1972	54
4-2	Percentage of Whites Who Were Strong Party Identifiers from 1952 Through 1972, by Years of Birth	57
4-3	Percentage of Whites Who Were Strong or Weak Party Identifiers from 1952 Through 1972, by Years of Birth	58
4-4	Percentage of Whites Who Were Independents with No Party Leanings from 1952 Through 1972, by Years of Birth	59
4-5	Party Identification Among Blacks from 1952 Through 1972	66

4-6	Percentage of Blacks Who Identified as Strong or Weak Republicans from 1952 Through 1972, by Years of Birth	68
5-1	Distribution of Respondents in 1970, by Level of Education, Years of Birth, and Race	79
5-2	Distribution of Respondents in 1972, by Level of Education, Years of Birth, and Race	80
5-3	Political Attitudes in 1970, by Level of Education, Years of Birth, and Race	81
5-4	Political Attitudes in 1972, by Level of Education, Years of Birth, and Race	82
5-5	Feelings Toward Groups in 1970, by Race	87
5-6	Feelings Toward Groups in 1972, by Race	87
5-7	Feelings Toward Groups in 1970, by Level of Education, Years of Birth, and Race	89
5-8	Feelings Toward Groups in 1972, by Level of Education, Years of Birth, and Race	92
6-1	Percentage of White Major-Party Voters Who Voted for McGovern in 1972, by Attitudes Toward Policy Questions	101
6-2	Percentage of White Major-Party Voters Who Voted for McGovern in 1972, by Feelings Toward Groups	102
6-3	Relationship Between Attitudes and Direction of Presidential Vote Among Whites in 1972, by Level of Education and Years of Birth	105
6-4	Relationship Between Feelings Toward Groups and Direction of Presidential Vote Among Whites in 1972, by Level of Education and Years of Birth	106

6-5	Relationship Between Attitudes and Direction of Party Identification Among Whites in 1970, by Level of Education and Years of Birth	111
6-6	Relationship Between Attitudes and Direction of Party Identification Among Whites in 1972, by Level of Education and Years of Birth	112
6-7	Relationship Between Feelings Toward Groups and Direction of Party Identification Among Whites in 1970, by Level of Education and Years of Birth	113
6-8	Relationship Between Feelings Toward Groups and Direction of Party Identification Among Whites in 1972, by Level of Education and Years of Birth	116

Preface

Birth, aging, and death gradually change the membership of any society. New generations supplant the old, but transforming the population need not lead to social change. The young may much resemble the old in their attitudes and behavior, and even when young persons differ from their elders, they may come to resemble them when they themselves age.

But though each generation perpetuates society, it may also change it. If the young could be isolated from their elders, it would be easier to create a new social order, and thus Plato argued that philosophers could establish the ideal polity more quickly if they expelled all citizens above the age of ten from the republic. At times a generation may be too corrupt to create a new order. The Book of Numbers relates that the generation freed from Egypt, which again and again showed its faithlessness, was condemned to have its carcasses consumed in the wilderness until a new generation, born in freedom, was reared to conquer Canaan.

But generational change is seldom this dramatic, and this study examines far less drastic changes than those proposed by Plato or related in the Books of Moses. Rather, we will examine the changes brought about by millions of Americans who became adults after the Great Depression. These citizens, who entered the electorate after World War II, did not lead America into a promised land, but they have transformed the political party system.

This book begins by examining the formation of the New Deal coalition that provided the basis for Democratic presidential majorities. That coalition, we will show, depended heavily upon support from working-class whites, that is to say, from blue-collar workers and their dependents. Then, we will examine the declining importance of social class upon party choice, as well as the mass mobilization of blacks into the electorate, which have transformed the social composition of the Democratic presidential coalition. The mass mobilization of blacks occurred among all age groups, but the decline of class-based voting among whites largely results from generational change. By analyzing age-group differences, we will demonstrate that the changing class composition of the Democratic presidential coalition was caused largely by new voters entering the electorate. By testing alternative explanations for age-group differences, we will develop a firmer basis for predicting the future composition of the Democratic presidential coalition, and, more important, will examine a process through which partisan alignments change. Then, we will examine the declining strength of party identification among the white electorate, and, through an analysis of age-group differences, show that this erosion also results from generational change. Lastly, we will demonstrate that the attitudinal basis for an alignment between upper-stratum whites and blacks may be emerging. By analyzing age-group differences among whites at differing educational levels, we will demonstrate that the Democrats are deeply divided and will point to difficulties they may face in rebuilding a successful presidential coalition.

This study relies heavily upon surveys conducted by the Survey Research Center of the University of Michigan, which were made available for analysis through the Inter-University Consortium for Political Research. I am grateful for the Consortium's cooperation, but the Consortium is not responsible for my analyses or interpretations. The study was funded partly by a Ford Foundation Faculty Research Fellowship during the academic year 1972-73, but the Ford Foundation is not responsible for my conclusions. The Department of Political Science and the Computer Institute for Social Science Research, Michigan State University, provided support. Thomas Jukam, my research assistant for two years during this project, helped greatly with the data analysis. Carol Thompson assisted me during the academic year 1973-74. I am especially grateful to Victor Hanby and Frank Pinner, who commented on the entire manuscript. John Aldrich, Paul Allen Beck, Bruce Bueno de Mesquita, Bruce Campbell, Neal Cutler, David Elkins, Ada Finifter, Alan Grimes, Nancy Hammond, Karen Oppenheim Mason, Warren Miller, Elizabeth Powell, David Rohde, and Joseph Schlesinger commented on portions of this study. My wife, Janet, helped me edit the manuscript, and, more important, provided encouragement.

Portions of Chapter 2 originally appeared in my, "The Democratic Party in search of whites," *New Society*, 30 (17 October 1974), pp. 138-139 and a large part of Chapter 3 originally appeared as my, "Generational Change in American Electoral Behavior," *American Political Science Review*, 68 (March 1974), pp. 93-105.

1 Forming the New Deal Coalition

Andrew Jackson founded the Democratic party after his defeat in 1824. Since then, the party has won 17 of 37 presidential elections. Although its initial victories were due to Jackson's personal popularity, the long-run success was built upon a coalition of agricultural interests that competed with commercial and nascent industrial interests. These economic forces translated into sectional alignments. The Democrats gained support from the South and West; their opposition came from the Northeast.

Jackson's coalition was also built upon a brilliant institutional mechanism—the party nominating convention. The founding fathers had devised a presidential selection procedure designed to minimize popular control. Electors, chosen from each state in a manner to be specified by its state legislature, would cast two votes, one of which was to be for a person who was not a resident of the elector's home state. Failing a majority of the electoral votes, which would be difficult to attain, the House of Representatives, with each state delegation casting one vote, would choose a president from among the five persons receiving the most electoral votes. These rules were modified after the 1800 election in which Jefferson and Burr, running together, received the same number of votes. Although Jefferson was clearly the presidential candidate, Burr the vice-presidential, the House procedure was necessary to choose Jefferson. The Twelfth Amendment specified that electors would designate which of their two votes was for president, which for vice-president; the House was now restricted to choosing from among the top three persons if no one succeeded in winning a majority.

But this reform did little to increase the likelihood that a single candidate would receive a majority of the electoral votes. The Democratic-Republicans managed to elect presidents, largely because of Jefferson's efforts in forming a rudimentary party. By 1820 the Federalists ceased to field a candidate, and Monroe ran unopposed. But the Democratic-Republicans had no clearly established rules for selecting presidential candidates, and the congressional caucus emerged as a nominating device. The caucus was effective in 1816, when it chose Monroe, but by 1824 it was unable to impose its choice upon the states. The caucus chose William Crawford, while various state legislatures nominated Clay, Jackson, Adams, and Calhoun. Calhoun withdrew to support Jackson, and in the four-way contest, Jackson received a plurality of both the popular and electoral vote. The House of Representatives chose Adams, who had run second. Adams's selection of Clay as his secretary of state led Jackson to charge that an "unholy alliance" had been formed against him.

Jackson campaigned for the presidency for the next three years, and after his victory in 1828 was determined to wrest from Congress control of the nominating process. The national party convention, a meeting of state notables, would agree upon a single candidate to be supported by Democratic electors in all states. Although the nomination process was not legally binding, it was politically effective, for candidates denied the national party nomination had no chance of winning. In one sense the party convention system has been supremely successful—the House of Representatives has not selected a president since 1824. Since 1828 the national parties have existed mainly to select presidential candidates, and Congress, and often congressmen themselves, have but a small voice in that process.

However brilliant the nominating convention device, it did not guarantee Democratic victories, for the opposition used the same mechanism to select their candidates. The sectional coalition organized by Jackson was difficult to defeat, and the anti-Jackson Whigs often selected war heroes to contend against it. But the Democratic coalition had a basic weakness, for southerners and westerners could not agree about the extension of slavery into the territories. "*La présence des noirs sur le sol des Etats-Unis*"[1] broke the Democratic party, and by 1860 the Democrats could not agree upon a candidate. A party convention at Charleston failed to nominate a candidate after 57 ballots. A second convention in Baltimore nominated Douglas, while southern bolters, who also met in Baltimore, nominated Breckinridge as the National Democratic candidate. With the Democrats divided, the Republicans were able to capture a majority of the electoral vote, in spite of winning only 40 percent of the popular vote.

By 1876 the Democrats captured a plurality of the popular vote, and were one vote short of a majority of the electoral vote. In 1884 they regained the presidency, mainly by revitalizing the South-West sectional coalition. But although politics was largely sectional, in most states, party competition was close. Unfortunately, we have scant data on the group basis of party support. It seems unlikely, however, that the industrial working class disproportionately supported the Democrats. The working class was composed largely of recent immigrants with little political sophistication. Within cities, machine politics, based more on local payoffs than class conflict, predominated. Ethnic groups often had strong partisan loyalties, although those loyalties might vary from city to city. Religion could become an issue, as Republicans discovered after condemning the Democrats as the party of "Rum, Romanism, and Rebellion." But the working class was so largely foreign, and so highly parochial, that it was difficult to organize even for economic gains. The most successful craft unions were largely apolitical.

While industrial workers were difficult to organize, the conflict between the industrialists and farmers intensified. Farmers, especially in the West, were squeezed by high railroad rates and by deflation. The Populists demanded relief, most notably by free coinage of silver that would cheapen money and lighten the debts on their heavily mortgaged farms. Although the Populists attempted to gain support from factory workers in the East, their appeals met with little success. Their blatant nativism was culturally unpalatable to many Catholic workers. Moreover, free silver was no panacea for the factory worker, for it would cheapen the value of his wages. As James L. Sundquist wrote, "Bryan's campaign polarized sentiment on what, for his purposes, was the wrong basis. He did not set class against class; he set rural against urban."[2] Yet, the Populists seriously threatened the eastern bankers and industrialists, especially after they captured the Democratic party at the 1896 convention. In factories throughout the East, workers were told not to return to work if Bryan were elected.

After Bryan's nomination in 1896 the Democrats lost seven of the next nine elections. The Republican ascendancy depended upon regional politics, in which they captured the eastern states, as well as most of the midwestern and western states. The South seemed permanently aligned with the Democratic party. E.E. Schattschneider estimated that by 1904 there were only six states in which the parties were evenly matched, and 30 in which there was virtually no party competition.[3]

Along with the intensification of sectional politics, there was a massive decline in turnout. In part, the absence of party competition may have discouraged persons from participating, but many voters were actually disfranchised. The period between 1896 and 1904 produced a striking exception to deTocqueville's classic maxim that once the franchise is expanded, pressures inevitably will rise to broaden the suffrage.

The mass disfranchisements in the South were aimed against blacks, but as the Fifteenth Amendment made it unconstitutional to disfranchise specifically on the basis of race, it was difficult to keep blacks away from the polls without also denying the ballot to poor whites. There was far from universal enthusiasm for denying blacks the ballot. Legislation to disfranchise blacks was supported mainly by whites from the black belt, and was often resisted by whites from areas with few blacks. In many southern states, legislation to restrict the ballot passed by only a narrow margin. Once blacks were denied the ballot, electoral competition between the parties vanished, and, as a consequence, participation fell among whites as well.[4]

The motives for restricting the franchise in the North are more difficult to interpret. Walter Dean Burnham argues that registration requirements, as well as making citizenship a condition of voting, were introduced to protect business interests against the threat of an emerging working class.[5] Others, such as Philip E. Converse, stress the desire to curb electoral fraud as a motivating force.[6] Regardless of the reasons for suffrage restrictions, their effect was clear. Voting declined markedly.

The Populist capture of the Democratic party, as well as the disfranchisement of southern blacks, left southern Populists with no choice but to compete within the Democratic party. In the process, southern and western Populists were isolated from each other.[7] The southern Democrats were content to abandon the presidency as long as the federal government covertly agreed to allow white domination in the South. Republican control of the White House was broken in 1912 only because the Republicans were divided between Taft and Roosevelt, and Wilson was able to win with only 42 percent of the popular vote. Wilson was reelected by a narrow margin in 1916 because he had kept the country out of war. But Wilson did little to alter the base of the Democratic presidential coalition. His social policies were less progressive than Roosevelt's and he bears the added ignominy of ordering racial segregation for the Washington bureaucracy.

The return to "normalcy" after World War I brought the Republicans to power for three elections. Harding, Coolidge, and Hoover all won by landslides; yet turnout was remarkably low.[a] Table 1-1 presents the percentage of adults that voted for each major candidate between 1920 and 1972, and the data demonstrate the inability of the Democrats to mobilize support in 1920 and 1924. In 1920 only 15 percent voted for Cox; in 1924 less than 13 percent supported Davis. But in 1928, when the Democrats nominated a Catholic, their support jumped by two-thirds, although, unfortunately for them, Republican support jumped as well. The Republican hegemony seemed assured, as did the American future. In accepting the Republican nomination in 1928, Hoover proclaimed, "We in America today are nearer to the final triumph over poverty than ever before in the history of any land." Hoover's assertion was premature, and by 1932, voters, weary of assurances that prosperity was just around the corner, were ready to throw the Republicans from office.

The Depression and the Emergence of Class Voting

The Depression made party realignment all but inevitable. New alignments emerged, but there was also continuity. No third party was successful and both major parties survived. And in spite of social unrest there was only a small increase in political participation.

Participation rates did not rise between 1928 and 1932, although they rose five percent in 1936 (see Table 1-1). Yet, in each of Roosevelt's victories, at least 40 percent of the adults failed to vote, and nonvoters always made up a clear plurality of the adult population. Southern blacks were the most conspicuously

---

[a]According to data compiled by Burnham, turnout in 1920 and 1924 was lower than in any presidential elections between 1828 and 1916. (See The Freedom to Vote Task Force, Democratic National Committee, *That All May Vote* [16 December 1969], Appendix III.) The extraordinarily low turnout in these years partly results from the Nineteenth Amendment that was ratified in August 1920. Nineteen-twenty is the first presidential election in which women are included in the total of adults upon which turnout percentages are based.

Table 1-1
Percentage of Adults Who Voted for Each Major Candidate Between 1920 and 1972

Year of Election:[a]	Democratic Candidate	Republican Candidate	Other Candidates	Did Not Vote	Total Percent	Voting Age Population
1920	15.10	*26.66*	2.45	55.79	100%	60,581,000
1924	12.79	*23.97*	7.60	55.64	100%	65,597,000
1928	21.34	*30.46*	0.52	47.68	100%	70,362,000
1932	*30.40*	21.00	1.55	47.05	100%	75,048,000
1936	*34.96*	21.01	1.53	42.50	100%	79,375,000
1940	*32.71*	26.74	0.28	40.36	100%	83,512,000
1944	*28.61*	24.60	0.38	46.41	100%	89,517,000
1948	*25.59*	23.28	2.78	48.35	100%	94,470,000
1952	27.59	*34.27*	0.30	37.84	100%	99,016,000
1956	25.11	*34.35*	0.40	40.14	100%	103,625,000
1960	*31.70*	31.60	0.18	36.52	100%	107,949,000
1964	*37.86*	23.85	0.30	37.99	100%	113,931,000
1968	26.06	*26.49*	8.46	38.99	100%	120,006,000
1972	20.89	*33.78*	0.99	44.34	100%	139,642,000

[a]Winning party in italics.

Source: Estimates of the voting age population from 1920 through 1968 were based upon *Politics in America: Edition IV* (Washington, D.C.: Congressional Quarterly, 1971), p. 74. The estimate of the voting age population in 1972 was based upon *The 1974 Elections* (Washington, D.C.: Congressional Quarterly, Supplement to *Congressional Quarterly Weekly Report*, 32 [February 23, 1974], p. 440). In calculating the percentage of the total adult population that voted for each candidate from 1920 through 1944, I relied upon statistics reported in Svend Petersen, *A Statistical History of the American Presidential Elections* (New York: Frederick Ungar, 1968). For calculating the percentage of votes received from 1948 through 1968, I relied upon *Politics in America*, Edition IV. For the 1972 election, I used *The 1974 Elections*, p. 440.

unmobilized group. Roosevelt avoided policies that might cost him white southern support, and throughout his presidency, the South remained solidly Democratic. Yet, sectional politics was already waning, for in none of Roosevelt's victories was the South a necessary part of a winning coalition.

As sectional politics declined, class-based politics emerged. The class basis of the New Deal coalition cannot be examined in detail, for the coalition was formed before social scientists trained in random sampling techniques began to study electoral behavior. It is clear, though, that Roosevelt in 1932 did little to mobilize class-based support. His only major promise was to support prohibition repeal. In his acceptance speech before the Democrats in Chicago, Roosevelt pledged a "new deal" for the American people, and throughout his campaign strongly suggested that he would use the federal government to improve economic conditions. But if Roosevelt intended that the government under his leadership was to be active, he left the content of that activism obscure.

Even during the first few years of his presidency Roosevelt did little to divide the electorate along class lines. Roosevelt, according to William E. Leuchtenburg, was more interested in the agricultural sector than the problems of urban, industrialized America, and much of the early New Deal legislation was aimed at improving the plight of the farmer.[8] Roosevelt only reluctantly supported legislation to aid the emerging industrial unions, and the National Labor Relations Act, passed in 1935, originated in Congress. By 1936, however, Roosevelt had abandoned his faith in an "all-class alliance," and directly attacked the monied interests.[9] The forces of "organized money," Roosevelt proclaimed at a Madison Square Garden campaign rally, "are unanimous in their hate for me—and I welcome their hatred. . . . I should like to have it said of my first administration that in it the forces of selfishness and of lust for power met their match. . . . I should like to have it said of my second administration that in it these forces met their master." Roosevelt received sizable financial support from trade unions, especially from the newly formed CIO. Yet, although economic issues were beginning to polarize the electorate along social class lines, Roosevelt still enjoyed sizable middle-class support. Leuchtenburg argues that Roosevelt's attempt to expand the Supreme Court, as well as his sympathy for the sit-down strikes, eroded middle-class support for the New Deal.[10]

Available data suggest that the class basis of the Democratic coalition emerged after 1932. Admittedly, Smith's candidacy in 1928 had attracted heavy Catholic support, and Catholics were disproportionately working class. Yet, in 1932 the Roosevelt landslide probably attracted persons from all social groups, and there is some evidence that class was not related to party choice. The best evidence can be found in the *Literary Digest* polls. These polls were based upon names in telephone books and lists of automobile owners, and, therefore, during the Depression years, heavily overrepresented upper-income groups. In 1932, though, the *Literary Digest* closely predicted the actual result. According to the *Digest*, Roosevelt would receive 56 percent of the vote; in fact, he received 57 percent. That the *Digest* results closely approximated the actual results strongly suggests that income differences were not related to party choice. In 1936 the *Digest* repeated its same biased sampling procedures and predicted that Roosevelt would receive 41 percent of the vote; in fact, he received 61 percent. This strongly suggests that class differences in voting occurred in 1936, and that these differences emerged after the 1932 election.[11]

Nineteen-thirty-six is the first year for which large-scale quota surveys are available, and these studies show considerable class polarization, in spite of relatively high levels of middle-class support for the Democrats. The most comprehensive analyses of survey data from this period have been conducted by Robert R. Alford[12] and by Norval D. Glenn.[13] Alford found that about 65 percent of the manually employed voters supported Roosevelt, whereas just under 50 percent of the nonmanually employed did.[b] A simple measure of class voting, computed by subtracting the percentage of nonmanually employed voters who voted Democratic from the percentage of manually employed voters who voted Democratic, yields an index of +16. Glenn reports the percentage of voters who voted Republican, and found that only 22 percent of the manually employed whites and their dependents voted for Landon, whereas 43 percent of the nonmanually employed did.[c] Class voting, based upon Glenn's analysis, was +21.[d] In 1940 Alford found only minimal changes in the percentage of manually employed who voted for Roosevelt, but among the nonmanually employed the proportion dropped to 40 percent. Class voting was +25. Glenn, on the other hand, shows a shift toward the Republicans among both classes; among working-class white voters, 31 percent voted Republican; among middle-class voters, 49 percent did. Class voting, according to Glenn, was +17.

The class basis of Roosevelt's support persisted even during the war-time election of 1944. The war provided a basis for national appeals that transcended class divisions, and neither candidate stressed economic issues. Surprisingly, class voting was about as high in 1944 as in 1940. Alford reports data from three separate surveys, but in one he misclassifies service workers as middle class, and thus underestimates class voting.[e] In one survey, Alford found that 59 percent of the manual workers voted for Roosevelt, whereas 41 percent of the middle-class voters did. In another, Alford found that 67 percent of the

---

[b]Alford does not control for race, but as only a small percentage of blacks voted, his inclusion of blacks probably has little effect on his results.

[c]Glenn explicitly notes that he classifies respondents according to the head of household's occupation. Alford apparently also uses this method of classification with most of his analyses, but he is less explicit about his procedures.

[d]This is reduced to +18 if one corrects for the underrepresentation of the South in early Gallup surveys. See Glenn, "Class and Party Support in 1972," mimeo, 1973, Table 1.

[e]In his analysis of the 1944 NORC survey, Alford classifies service workers as working class. I also analyzed this survey. Although the NORC does not explain what jobs service workers performed, I was able to cross-tabulate their measure of the head of household's occupation with another measure of economic level contained within the survey. Service workers tend to be classified as poor. With other surveys, Alford does classify service workers as working class.

working-class voters supported Roosevelt, whereas 46 percent of the middle-class voters did. Class voting, according to Alford's calculations, was +18 and +21 in these two surveys. Glenn combined the results of several surveys and found that 31 percent of the working-class whites voted Republican, whereas 48 percent of the middle-class whites did; class voting, according to Glenn's analysis, was +17.[f] My own analysis of the 1944 National Opinion Research Center survey of the civilian electorate, presented in Table 1-2, shows that 64 percent of the white working-class major-party voters supported Roosevelt, whereas 45 percent of the white middle-class major-party voters did. Class voting, according to my calculations, was +19.

On balance, available data show a substantial level of class voting in 1936, 1940, and 1944. While class voting was not high compared with levels of class polarization in Britain, Australia, New Zealand, or Scandinavia, Roosevelt's victories depended heavily on high levels of working-class support. These data strongly suggest that after 1936, Roosevelt won by gaining most of the blue-collar votes while gaining less than half of the white-collar votes.

Blacks and the New Deal Coalition

Blacks were not a major part of the New Deal coalition, for participation among blacks was low and Roosevelt did little to mobilize black votes. Most blacks lived

Table 1-2
How Voted for President in 1944, by Social Class and Race[a]

Race:	White			Black		
Social Class:	Working Class	Middle Class	Class Voting[b] Among Whites	Working Class	Middle Class	Class Voting Among Blacks
Democratic	63.1%	44.3%	+19	89.7%	65.2%	+24
Republican	36.1	55.1		10.3	34.8	
Other Party	0.8	0.6		0.0	0.0	
Total Percent	100.0	100.0		100.0	100.0	
(Number)	(604)	(681)		(29)	(23)	

[a]Based upon a quota sample of the civilian electorate by the National Opinion Research Center. "White-collar" workers and their dependents are classified as middle class; "manual" and "service" workers as working class. Farmers are excluded from the analysis. The direction of vote is based upon the way each respondent said he or she voted in a survey conducted shortly after the election. Southern blacks were not included in the survey. In Table 2-1, Chapter 2, I present the percentage that did not vote, but I have not included nonvoters in Table 1-2 because the 1944 survey cannot be used to estimate levels of voting among the large proportion of males that was in the armed forces. In addition, it cannot be used to estimate participation levels among blacks.

[b]Class voting is the percentage of working-class respondents who voted Democratic minus the percentage of middle-class respondents who voted Democratic. (Based on major-party voters.)

---

[f]This is reduced to +16 if one corrects for the underrepresentation of the South.

in the South and were denied the franchise through both quasilegal and illegal stratagems. The federal government made no effort to enforce the Fifteenth Amendment. According to estimates by Ralph Bunch, only 80,000 to 90,000 of the 3,600,000 blacks who lived in Alabama, Georgia, Mississippi, Louisiana, Florida, Texas, South Carolina, and Arkansas voted in the 1940 presidential election.[14]

Among blacks who did vote, the Democrats made consistent gains after 1932. In 1932 most blacks, in spite of dissatisfaction with Hoover, remained loyal to the party of Lincoln. Black leaders criticized early New Deal policies. The National Recovery Act, they argued, displaced black workers, and the Agricultural Readjustment Act drove black tenants and sharecroppers from the land. Yet, blacks did benefit from some New Deal policies, especially from relief. By 1934 blacks were beginning to move toward the Democrats, and by 1936 a majority voted for Roosevelt. According to a *Fortune* poll conducted in 1938, 85 percent of the black respondents considered themselves pro-Roosevelt.[15] Gunnar Myrdal analyzed data from 15 predominantly black wards in nine northern cities and found that Roosevelt carried four in 1932, nine in 1936, and fourteen in 1940.[16]

Myrdal, writing in 1944, concluded that blacks had discarded their traditional allegiances to the Republicans, disdained third parties, and would remain flexible in their partisan loyalties. "Neither the Republican party nor the Democratic party," he predicted, "will be certain of the Negro vote for any length of time without real exertions."[17] Myrdal also reported that blacks, like whites, displayed class differentials in their support for the Democrats: Blacks in lower economic groups were more likely to vote Democratic than those in upper groups.[18]

My own analysis of the 1944 National Opinion Research Center (NORC) survey (see Table 1-2) shows that nearly four out of five black voters supported Roosevelt. Among blacks, as among whites, blue-collar workers were more likely to vote Democratic than were white-collar workers; class voting among blacks was +24. But racial differences were also sharp. Blacks were 25 percent more likely to vote Democratic than whites were.[g]

A social group's contribution to an electoral coalition depends not only upon its loyalty to the party, but also upon its size and its turnout.[19] As long as blacks lived mainly in the South, and as long as they were disfranchised, they could contribute little to the Democratic presidential coalition. The data in Table 1-2, which adequately represent nonsouthern blacks, suggest that even by 1944, Roosevelt received only about one in 18 of his votes from blacks. Roosevelt did not depend upon the black vote, and never exerted great efforts to gain it.

Notes

1. Alexis de Tocqueville, *De la Démocratie en Amérique* (Paris: Union Générale d'Éditions, 1963), p. 342. "If ever America undergoes great revolu-

---
[g]Based upon respondents included in Table 1-2.

tions," de Tocqueville wrote in 1840, "they will be brought about by the presence of the black race on the soil of the United States; that is to say, they will owe their origin, not to the equality, but to the inequality of condition." *Democracy in America*, Volume II, Phillips Bradley, ed., (New York: Vintage Books, 1945), p. 270.

2. James L. Sundquist, *Dynamics of the Party System: Alignment and Realignment of Political Parties in the United States* (Washington, D.C.: The Brookings Institution, 1973), p. 149.

3. E.E. Schattschneider, *The Semisovereign People: A Realist's View of Democracy in America* (New York: Holt, Rinehart, and Winston, 1960), p. 83.

4. V.O. Key, Jr., *Southern Politics in State and Nation* (New York: Knopf, 1949), pp. 533-54.

5. See Walter Dean Burnham, "The Changing Shape of the American Political Universe," *American Political Science Review* 59 (March 1965): 7-28; and Burnham, *Critical Elections and the Mainsprings of American Politics* (New York: Norton, 1970), pp. 71-90.

6. Philip E. Converse, "Change in the American Electorate," in Angus Campbell and Converse, eds., *The Human Meaning of Social Change* (New York: Russell Sage, 1972), pp. 266-301.

7. Both Schattschneider and Key make this argument. See, *The Semisovereign People*, pp. 79-83 and *Southern Politics*, pp. 551-54.

8. William E. Leuchtenburg, *Franklin D. Roosevelt and the New Deal: 1932-1940* (New York: Harper and Row, 1963), p. 35.

9. Ibid., p. 183.

10. Ibid., p. 243.

11. For a brief discussion of these polls, see Julian L. Simon, *Basic Research Methods in Social Science: The Art of Empirical Investigation* (New York: Random House, 1969), pp. 111-15. Both Burnham and Sundquist point to the *Literary Digest* polls as evidence that class-based voting emerged after the 1932 election. (See *Critical Elections*, p. 56, and *Dynamics of the Party System*, p. 203.)

12. Robert R. Alford, *Party and Society: The Anglo-American Democracies* (Chicago: Rand McNally, 1963), pp. 352-53.

13. Norval D. Glenn, "Class and Party Support in the United States: Recent and Emerging Trends," *Public Opinion Quarterly* 37 (Spring 1973): 1-20.

14. Cited in Gunnar Myrdal, *An American Dilemma: The Negro Problem and Modern Democracy* (New York: Harper and Row, 1962), p. 475.

15. Cited in Leuchtenburg, *Franklin Roosevelt*, p. 187.

16. Myrdal, *An American Dilemma*, pp. 495-96.

17. Ibid., p. 505.

18. Ibid., pp. 495-97.

19. See Robert Axelrod, "Where the Votes Come From: An Analysis of Electoral Coalitions: 1952-1968," *American Political Science Review* 66 (March 1972): 11-20.

2

The Decline of Class-Based Politics in Postwar America

The New Deal coalition was based largely upon social-class cleavages. As I will document, class-based partisan voting eroded markedly during the postwar years. The relationship of social class to partisan preference has been diminishing in other advanced industrial societies as well, and one factor common to them all is unprecedented prosperity since World War II.

Prosperity erodes class conflicts for many reasons. In an advanced industrial society the differences in rewards received by the working class and the middle class are reduced, largely because the literacy skills required for middle-class jobs become less scarce and, therefore, less valuable on the labor market.[1] Differences in life-style, formerly linked with visible signs of status, are reduced. Class conflict becomes institutionalized, as working-class demands are channeled through legitimate (and increasingly conservative) trade unions. As the middle class expands, Left parties abandon or play down direct appeals to the working class in an attempt to gain middle-class support. All these factors tend to reduce the relationship between social class and partisan choice.

These broad generalizations must be qualified when we discuss specific countries. In Britain, where that relationship is especially strong, and where there are few social bases for cross-cutting cleavages, the relationship between class and party choice tends to persist, in spite of social and economic changes; yet, even in Britain, class-based partisanship declined during the 1960s.[2] In Canada ethnic and linguistic cleavages are so intense that class-based partisan politics have not arisen at the national level. And the United States is unlike any other advanced industrial society, because the U.S. has a large number of blacks.

Economic and Social Changes in Postwar America

To what extent has prosperity affected the United States? That Americans have experienced unprecedented prosperity seems almost unquestionable. Between 1950 and 1970 the per-capita gross national product rose (in 1958 constant dollars) from $2,340 to $3,750 and per-capita disposable income rose from $1,650 to $2,660.[3] Of course, this income was not shared equally, and some evidence suggests that the distribution pattern for the entire population does not differ much from that in the 1950s or even the 1920s.[4] But in absolute terms, most social groups improved their positions during the postwar years.

Most important for our analysis is the increasing similarity in incomes between blue-collar and white-collar workers.[5] This trend occurred partly because the literacy skills necessary to perform white-collar jobs became more widespread, and partly because blue-collar workers organized more effectively. In addition, automation, especially computer technology, has rendered many semiskilled (and some skilled) white-collar jobs superfluous. Yet, the convergence of income between the classes should not be exaggerated. It occurred mainly because of the relatively slow income growth among clerical and sales workers. Professional and managerial employees have maintained, and often increased, their relative advantage over the manually employed.

Life-style differences between the classes, when measured by consumption patterns, have declined. Cars, televisions, washing machines, telephones, and refrigerators are now widely owned. Profound cultural differences remain between the working class and the upper-middle class, but the most visible differences have blurred.

Judging the degree to which class conflicts have become institutionalized is more difficult. Unions are now legally recognized, and are encouraged by most federal legislation. Moreover, throughout most of the United States, unions are now accepted as the normal mechanism for representing workers. Pockets of resistance to unionization remain, especially in the South where "right to work" laws discourage organization. But major corporations do not challenge the legitimacy of unions, and strikes, though still common, do not involve the right to bargain collectively.

The middle class has grown, but we should not exaggerate this change. The middle class has grown mainly because of increasing numbers of women in the work force, for most women workers are nonmanually employed. Among men, the percentage of manual workers has not declined dramatically. Among nonagriculturally employed males, the percentage of manually employed declined from 70 percent in 1900 to 64 percent in 1950.[6] By 1972, 58 percent of the nonagriculturally employed males were manual workers.[7] According to data collected by the University of Michigan Survey Research Center, the major data base for this study, 55 percent of the nonagricultural white households in 1952 were headed by a manual worker; in 1972, 52 percent were. The American work force has changed far less than the prophets of the post-industrial society claim. These writers, such as Daniel Bell, point to the growing service sector.[8] By 1980, it is estimated, about 80 percent of all Americans will be employed in services. But most service workers perform unskilled or semiskilled manual labor, and have neither the job security nor career prospects often enjoyed by middle-class employees. Most service workers are best classified as working class.

While the nonagricultural sector changed gradually, the agricultural sector has been dramatically transformed. Twenty million Americans left the land between 1940 and 1970, an exodus that has been compared with the migrations in England during the Enclosures.[9] The agricultural sector contracted in European societies as well, but in the United States this decline was accompanied by racial migration. About one person in five who left the land was black. Blacks not only moved from the farms to the cities, but from the South to the North and West. In 1940 only 23 percent of the blacks lived outside the South; by 1970, 47 percent did. By 1970 four out of five blacks lived in metropolitan areas and blacks were more urbanized than whites.[10]

Class Voting in Postwar Presidential Elections

These economic and social changes contributed to a sharp decline in the relationship between social class and partisan choice, a change that has transformed the social composition of the Democratic presidential coalition. Angus Campbell and his colleagues recognized the declining relationship of class to party choice.[11] The authors of *The American Voter* developed a measure of "status polarization" to assess the relationship between occupational ranking and direction of partisanship. The greater the tendency of the lower occupational groups to vote Democratic and of the upper groups to vote Republican, the higher the measure of status polarization.[12] They found that status polarization had declined in the years following World War II and suggested that it would continue to remain low. "In view of the economic axis of class feelings," they write, "we would readily assume that status polarization should increase in time of depression, and decrease in periods of prosperity."[13] By examining changes in status polarization in postwar elections, they conclude:

The most striking feature of the polarization trend in the recent past has been the steady and rapid depolarization between 1948 and 1956. This decline occurred in a post-war period when the nation was enjoying a striking ascent to prosperity and a consequent release from the pressing economic concerns that had characterized the Depression.[14]

Campbell and his colleagues based their conclusions mainly upon an eight year time period, although they also examined some data from 1944. They acknowledged that data covering a longer period were necessary to reach more definitive conclusions. In his study of the changing relationship of social class to partisan choice, Alford examined data collected over 24 years.[15] Alford contested Campbell's conclusion that the relationship between social class and party choice was declining. He argued that in choosing 1948 as the starting point for a time-series analysis, Campbell and his colleagues had selected an atypical election. The relationship of social class to partisan choice was higher in 1948 than in any previous election for which survey data are available, and by using 1948 as the beginning of a time-series analysis, one may conclude incorrectly that the relationship of class to party is declining rapidly. Based upon his own analysis, Alford concluded "there has been no substantial shift in the class bases of American politics since the 1930's, despite the prosperity since World War II and despite the shifts to the Right in the Eisenhower era."[16]

My own analysis of data collected by the University of Michigan Survey Research Center strongly suggests that Campbell and his colleagues were correct in concluding that the relationship between class and party choice was declining. Alford would, I believe, have reached different conclusions if he had been able to examine voting behavior in the 1968 and 1972 elections, but he also erred, as we will see, by failing to examine systematically age-group differences. Table 2-1 shows how persons voted between 1948 and 1972, controlling for social class and race. (In all these surveys, the proportion that reported voting is higher than the actual turnout [see Table 1-1], but the data can be used as a rough guide to relative levels of participation among social groups.) Table 2-1 also presents levels of class voting among whites and among blacks in each election.[a] In Table 2-2, I have presented the percentage of white[b] major-party voters who voted Democratic among five occupational grades between 1948 and 1972. In addition, I have computed a measure of association between occupational ranking and direction of presidential vote using a Kendall's tau-c that closely approximates the statistical techniques used in *The American Voter*.[c] Following the Michigan authors, I have labeled this measure "status polarization." This measure has been criticized by Alford and by Walter Korpi.[17] Alford argues that, in addition to conceptual problems, the measure of status polarization is difficult to interpret. The "intermediate range" of status polarization—the range between 0 and 1—"is an extremely ambiguous one mainly because it covers a range of alternatives encompassing most of the possibilities for variation in a consensual parliamentary system."[18] Korpi reaches similar conclusions and argues that "Campbell's measure of class solidarity is neither informative nor useful since it only relates the political distinctiveness of class to an arbitrary baseline."[19]

Even if one accepts these criticisms, it is useful to report levels of status polarization, for this allows us to replicate and add to the work of the Michigan authors. Moreover, the measure of status polarization has some utility if one views the occupational hierarchy as stratified into several layers, for the Kendall's tau is a useful measure of ordinal relationships and allows one to avoid relying solely upon a dichotomous measure of occupation.

---

[a]Class voting is the percentage of working-class respondents who voted Democratic minus the percentage of middle-class respondents who voted Democratic. Calculations are based only upon major-party voters, although the effect of including Wallace voters in the analysis is reported below.

For a discussion of class voting, see Alford, *Party and Society*, pp. 79-86.

[b]Because there are very few blacks in the upper occupational grades, I have not reported the findings for blacks.

[c]Campbell and his colleagues used a tau-b to measure this relationship. It was impossible to replicate precisely the measure of occupational status used by the University of Michigan authors since there are some ambiguities in their description of their measure.

Table 2-1
How Voted for President Between 1948 and 1972, by Social Class and Race[a]

Race:	White			Black		
Social Class:	Working Class	Middle Class	Class Voting[b] Among Whites	Working Class	Middle Class	Class Voting Among Blacks
Year of Election:						
1948						
Democratic	46.1%	23.5%	+44	30.0%	(1)	
Republican	15.1	51.4		10.0	(3)	
Other Party	1.8	1.1		0.0	0	
Did Not Vote	34.2	21.9		56.7	(2)	
Other Response[c]	2.7	2.2		3.3	(2)	
Total Percent (Number)	99.9 (219)	100.1 (183)		100.0 (30)	(8)	
1952						
Democratic	38.6%	26.8%	+20	27.8%	36.8%	+11
Republican	36.6	59.4		6.5	15.8	
Other Party	0.3	0.2		0.0	0.0	
Did Not Vote	23.8	12.8		65.7	42.1	
Other Response[c]	0.7	0.8		0.0	5.3	
Total Percent (Number)	100.0 (614)	100.0 (507)		100.0 (108)	100.0 (19)	
1956						
Democratic	29.9%	29.0%	+8	26.8%	13.3%	+48
Republican	39.7	54.6		9.8	40.0	
Other Party	0.1	0.5		0.0	0.0	

Table 2-1(cont.)

Race: Social Class:	White Working Class	White Middle Class	Class Voting[b] Among Whites	Black Working Class	Black Middle Class	Class Voting Among Blacks
Did Not Vote	29.1	15.3		62.5	46.7	
Other Response[c]	1.2	0.5		0.9	0.0	
Total Percent (Number)	100.0 (763)	100.0 (568)		100.0 (112)	100.0 (15)	
1960						
Democratic	42.8%	39.8%	+12	39.8%	38.5%	+14
Republican	33.2	49.1		14.6	26.9	
Other Party	0.7	0.3		0.0	0.0	
Did Not Vote	22.7	9.7		39.8	34.6	
Other Response[c]	0.5	1.1		5.8	0.0	
Total Percent (Weighted N)	99.9 (761)	100.0 (631)		100.0 (103)	100.0 (26)	
1964						
Democratic	55.9%	46.6%	+19	61.2%	82.8%	0
Republican	19.0	37.3		0.0	0.0	
Other Party	0.2	0.0		0.0	0.0	
Did Not Vote	23.6	15.5		37.8	13.8	
Other Response[c]	1.2	0.6		1.0	3.4	
Total Percent (Number)	99.9 (567)	100.0 (541)		100.0 (98)	100.0 (29)	

1968						
Democratic	26.7%	28.4%	+10	65.2%	78.3%	+2
Republican	30.0	48.0		2.5	4.3	
American Independent Party	10.2	8.3		0.0	0.0	
Other Party	0.2	0.2		0.0	0.0	
Did Not Vote	27.3	10.9		27.5	17.4	
Other Response[c]	5.6	4.2		7.5	0.0	
Total Percent	100.0	100.0		100.0	100.0	
(Number)	(520)	(504)		(80)	(23)	
1972						
Democratic	19.9%	23.1%	+2	48.2%	70.9%	−13
Republican	44.3	55.6		10.8	3.6	
Other Party	0.3	0.9		0.0	0.0	
Did Not Vote	32.2	18.3		38.8	25.5	
Other Response[c]	3.3	2.1		2.2	0.0	
Total Percent	100.0	100.0		100.0	100.0	
(Number)	(915)	(858)		(139)	(55)	

[a]Surveys conducted by the University of Michigan Survey Research Center. Professionals, semiprofessionals, self-employed businessmen, managerial, supervisory, clerical, sales, and other white-collar workers were classified as middle class; skilled workers, semiskilled workers, unskilled workers, service workers, and protective service workers were classified as working class. Social class was defined by the head of household's occupation, or, if the head of household were not employed, by his or her occupation when he or she worked. Following procedures used by Alford, Glenn, and Campbell, et al., farmers have been excluded from the analysis. The direction of vote is based upon the way each respondent said he or she voted in a survey conducted shortly after the election.

[b]Class voting is the percentage of working-class respondents who voted Democratic minus the percentage of middle-class respondents who voted Democratic. (Based on major-party voters.)

[c]Refused to answer, would not say, did not know.

Table 2-2
Percentage of White Major-Party Voters Who Voted Democratic, by Occupational Level[a]

Occupational Level:	Professionals and Semiprofessionals	Self-Employed, Managerial, Supervisory	Clerical, Sales Other White Collar	Skilled and Semiskilled Workers	Unskilled Workers	Status Polarization[b]
Year of Election:						
1948	32% (31)[c]	14% (50)	46% (56)	77% (99)	71% (35)	.48
1952	27% (104)	33% (199)	32% (134)	51% (354)	51% (108)	.21
1956	24% (141)	39% (203)	40% (131)	44% (389)	41% (142)	.10
1960[d]	39% (176)	51% (189)	43% (196)	57% (435)	54% (144)	.12
1964	54% (121)	54% (195)	59% (138)	73% (326)	79% (99)	.21
1968	33% (163)	39% (119)	42% (103)	48% (242)	43% (53)	.12
1972	34% (275)	23% (225)	30% (175)	32% (470)	27% (117)	-.01

[a]My main goal in constructing Tables 2-1 and 2-2 was to maximize comparability over time and I followed the occupational categories used in the 1948 and 1952 surveys, even though more detailed categories could be used for subsequent surveys. For example, in both the 1948 and 1952 surveys, skilled and semiskilled workers were included under the same code, and, to maintain comparability, I grouped them together in subsequent years.
[b]Status polarization is the Kendall's tau-c relationship between a five-fold ordinal measure of occupation as listed above and direction of presidential vote (among major-party voters).
[c]Numbers in parentheses are the totals upon which percentages are based.
[d]Weighted Ns.

The data in Table 2-2 are also useful because they demonstrate the utility of the manual-nonmanual distinction. Richard F. Hamilton, after an extensive analysis of social class and politics in America, concludes that the manual-nonmanual dichotomy is not the most important occupational distinction in American politics. Rather, he argues, the most important distinction is between the lower-middle and the upper-middle classes. Hamilton considers this finding among the most significant in his entire book,[20] although he uses the manual-nonmanual dichotomy for most of his analysis. Hamilton's findings were based primarily upon the 1952, 1956, and 1964 Survey Research Center (SRC) surveys, but Hamilton focused upon party identification as his dependent variable. As the data in Table 2-2 demonstrate, the manual-nonmanual distinction is important in explaining voting behavior. Although skilled and semiskilled manual workers were not always much more Democratic than lower-grade nonmanual workers, the manual-nonmanual distinction was the most important behavioral cutting point in those elections where occupational ranking was related strongly to presidential vote (1948, 1952, and 1964).

Five basic facts emerge from the data. First there has been a substantial decline in the relationship between class and party during the postwar years. Admittedly, class voting was atypically high in 1948. But even if one uses 1952 as a starting point, overall levels of class voting have been declining. Class voting was +20 in 1952, and it approached this level in only one of the five subsequent elections (see Table 2-1). Status polarization was .21 in 1952; it was markedly lower in four of the five subsequent elections (see Table 2-2).

In 1972 there was virtually no relationship between class and party choice; among whites, professional workers were more likely to vote Democratic than was any other occupational group. While at first glance, 1972 seems unique, it may actually differ little from 1968. Class voting would be even lower in 1968 if Wallace voters were classified with Nixon voters, for Wallace drew disproportionate strength from the working class. Among white working-class voters, 15 percent voted for Wallace, among white middle-class voters, 10 percent did.[d] Including Wallace voters with the Republican voters would reduce class voting to +6, status polarization to .08. Such a classification might be reasonable, especially as Wallace voters who also voted in 1972 favored Nixon by a ratio of nearly four to one over McGovern.[e]

---

[d]As Hamilton notes, the 1968 SRC data show that the tendency of working-class voters to support Wallace more often than middle-class voters did, occurred only in the South. (See *Class and Politics*, p. 461.) Although I used somewhat different procedures than Hamilton, I obtained similar results. According to my analyses, eight percent of the white working-class nonsouthern voters ($n = 258$) voted for Wallace, whereas seven percent of the white middle-class nonsouthern voters ($n = 321$) did. In the South, 36 percent of the white working-class voters ($n = 91$) voted for Wallace, 20 percent of the white middle-class voters ($n = 107$) did. But Glenn, based upon an analysis of the combined results of five Gallup surveys conducted shortly after the 1968 election, found pronounced class differences in Wallace support in both the South and non-South. (See note g.)

[e]The 1972 SRC survey asked respondents how they had voted in 1968. Of the 130 whites who said they voted for Wallace in 1968 and who also voted for president in 1972, 75 percent voted for Nixon, 20 percent for McGovern, four percent for Schmitz, and one voted for another candidate.

Glenn's analyses, based upon Gallup data, also show a definite decline in class voting during the postwar years. According to Glenn, class voting averaged +17.6 between 1936 and 1948, fell to +10.6 in the two Eisenhower elections, and averaged +11.7 for the four post-Eisenhower elections.[f] Glenn found an even stronger tendency for the working class to support Wallace in 1968; 19 percent of the white working-class voters supported Wallace, 7 percent of the white middle-class voters did.[g] And, as with my analysis, Glenn found virtually no relationship between class and party choice in 1972. Combining five Gallup surveys, Glenn found that 71 percent of the middle-class whites voted for Nixon, whereas 68 percent of the working-class whites did; class voting was a negligible +2.6.[21]

Table 2-1 also shows a decline in class voting among blacks. Up through 1960, middle-class blacks voted Republican more often than working-class blacks. In 1964 virtually all blacks voted for Johnson; the Survey Research Center could find only one black among the nearly 400 they interviewed who had voted for Goldwater.[h] In 1968 virtually no blacks voted Republican. In 1972 about one black voter in seven supported Nixon. Yet, Nixon gained votes mainly from working-class blacks and class voting among blacks was −13.

The second basic fact demonstrated by these data is that the relationship of class to party has varied greatly, thus suggesting that party elites may affect that relationship by the strategies they employ.[i,22,23,24] Truman's whistle-stop

---

[f]Norval D. Glenn, "Class and Party Support in 1972," mimeo, 1973.

Glenn introduces controls for region and shows that, for some years, trends in the South differed from those in the rest of the United States. Alford, too, introduces controls for region.

I seldom discuss between-region differences for two reasons. First, while regional differences are sometimes interesting, the overall national trend is more important. The electorate, especially since the end of the Solid South, has become nationalized. In fact, from 1892 on, the presidential candidate with the most popular votes has been elected. Thus, a study of presidential coalition formation can concentrate on those groups that can contribute to a nationwide popular vote plurality.

But there is another reason for me to disregard regional analyses. When one conducts an analysis of age-group differences across time among persons in different regions, one faces severe methodological problems that are discussed on p. 39.

[g]Based upon my recalculation of data presented in Glenn, "Class and Party Support in the United States," 12 percent of the nonsouthern white working class ($n = 1399$) voted for Wallace, whereas among nonsouthern white middle-class voters ($n = 1521$), only four percent did. Among southern white working-class voters ($n = 301$), 49 percent voted for Wallace, among middle-class southern white voters ($n = 250$), 22 percent did.

[h]Table 2-1 reveals no black Goldwater voters, but in addition to the 159 blacks interviewed by the SRC as part of its random sample of the American electorate, 263 were interviewed as a supplementary sample. A total of 382 blacks were interviewed after the 1964 election. Of the 259 that voted, 256 voted for Johnson, one for Goldwater, and two refused to say how they voted.

[i]Glenn's analyses, however, do not show strong variations in levels of class voting from election to election. The main difference between his findings and mine is that I found marked increases in class voting in 1948 and 1964, whereas Glenn, using Gallup data, did not.

Whose results are correct? The SRC data for 1948 are probably more reliable than the

campaign exhorted the faithful to remember that the Democrats were the party of the little man. By promising to repeal the Taft-Hartley Act and to reestablish a Fair Employment Practices Commission, Truman appealed to the working class and to blacks. The relationship between class and party was high, for Truman captured three out of four working-class votes while gaining less than a third of the middle-class votes. Stevenson, on the other hand, avoided class-based appeals. Perhaps by 1952 it was too late for any Democrat to fuel a campaign train on memories of the breadlines, and Stevenson made no such attempt. As Richard F. Hamilton writes, "Early in the 1950s Democrats began to abandon their New Deal-Fair Deal focus. This was stimulated by the conclusions of liberal intellectuals who argued that those concerns were passé."[25] Admittedly, class voting was relatively high in 1952, but by 1956, when Stevenson again avoided economic issues, class voting was negligible.[26]

In 1960 Kennedy stressed party loyalties, while continually reminding voters that religion should not be an issue. Again class voting was low, even though Catholics, who overwhelmingly supported Kennedy, are more likely to be working class than are Protestants.[j] In 1964, on the other hand, class voting rose sharply, although this rise may have resulted more from Goldwater's economic conservatism than from Johnson's appeals. In 1968, when foreign policy and race-related issues became more salient, class voting again declined. In 1972, when the Democrats all but abandoned appeals to the working class in an attempt to mobilize youth, blacks, Chicanos, and women, working-class whites defected in record numbers and there was virtually no relationship between social class and party choice.

As the relationship of class to party choice varies greatly, class voting might rise in future elections, although the analysis to be presented in the next chapter strongly suggests that high levels of class voting will not recur. Yet, any projection will be influenced heavily by the last data point analyzed. Hamilton's analysis essentially stopped with an examination of the 1964 election and devoted little attention to the 1968 results. This may have led him to conclude that the relationship between class and party choice was likely to persist, and

---

Gallup, for until late 1952 Gallup surveys were based upon quota samples that underrepresented lower educational, income, and occupational levels, whereas the Michigan studies used random samples. The Gallup surveys for 1948 are particularly questionable. (See reference note 22.) Moreover, my finding that class was related strongly to party choice in 1948 is supported by Bernard R. Berelson's study of Elmira, N.Y., which found socio-economic status to be related strongly to presidential voting (see reference note 23), as well as Samuel Lubell's impressionistic findings (see reference note 24).

Even today, the Michigan researchers use better sampling procedures than Gallup, for Gallup still uses quota techniques, whereas the SRC uses random sampling procedures down to the level of selecting individuals within households. Most political scientists share my view that the SRC studies provide the best available time-series data.

[j]Over 80 percent of the Catholic voters supported Kennedy, and Kennedy fared only marginally better among working-class Catholics than among middle-class Catholics. But among white Protestants, Kennedy did better among the working class than among the middle class. Among white Protestant working-class major-party voters ($n = 374$), Kennedy received 41 percent of the vote, whereas among white Protestant middle-class major-party voters ($n = 405$), he received 31 percent. (Numbers for 1960 are weighted.)

might actually increase.²⁷ Accepting our view that political elites can affect greatly the relationship of class to party choice, makes one more cautious about predicting relationships.

A third fact also emerges from a closer examination of Table 2-1. Democrats have been more successful when the relationship between class and party has been high. The Democrats won two of the three postwar elections in which the relationship of class to party was high; they lost three of the four in which that relationship was low. The Democrats won two postwar elections, 1948 and 1960, with a majority of the white working-class vote and a minority of the middle-class vote; they lost only one election, 1952, in which they gained a majority of the working-class vote. In only one election, 1964, did the Democrats win most of the middle-class votes. In short, Democratic presidential candidates have depended upon attaining a majority of the blue-collar vote; when they have done so, they have almost always won; the Democrats have never won an election without obtaining a majority of the white working-class vote.

Fourthly, when viewed from another perspective, the data in Table 2-1 show that racial differences in voting behavior have been growing and that they are far more dramatic than those between classes. When we measure racial voting by subtracting the percentage of whites who voted Democratic from the percentage of blacks who voted Democratic, we find that in 1948 racial voting was only +9. In 1952, racial voting rose to +37, was +26 in 1956, but dropped to +19 in 1960. In 1964, in spite of Johnson's support among whites, racial voting rose to +35; in 1968 it was +54 (or +60 if Wallace voters are included with Nixon voters); in 1972, when Nixon gained some black support, racial voting was still +56.[k] This level of racial polarization far exceeds the relationship of most sociological variables to partisan choice, even when compared with voting behavior in some highly polarized European societies.

Lastly, Table 2-1 demonstrates that the most dramatic decline in Democratic support during the postwar years has been among working-class whites. This is illustrated more clearly if we examine the proportion of white working class and middle class major-party voters who supported the Democratic presidential candidate in each election, and these data, including our analysis of the 1944 election, are presented in Figure 2-1. Between 1944 and 1968 the Democrats suffered a 17 percent drop among working-class whites, a 7 percent drop among middle-class whites; between 1944 and 1972 working-class support for the Democrats dropped 33 percent, middle-class support declined 15 percent. There was a massive drop in working-class support between 1948 and 1968, while the Democrats gained among the middle class. Between 1952 and 1968 the Democrats suffered a 4 percent loss among working-class whites, while registering a 6 percent gain among the white middle class. Between 1952 and 1972 the

---
[k]Based upon respondents in Table 2-1. Racial voting is usually slightly higher if all persons, including those who are neither working nor middle class, are included in the analysis.

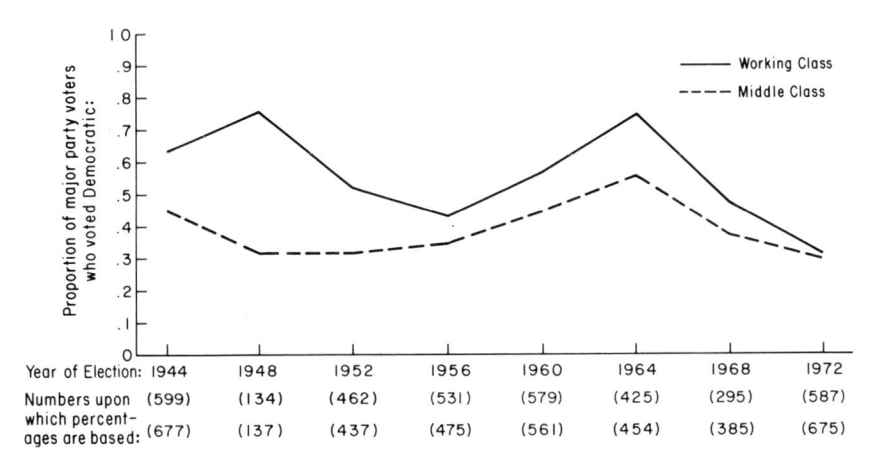

Figure 2-1. Proportion of White Major-Party Voters Who Voted Democratic for President from 1944 through 1972, by Social Class (Weighted N for 1960)

Democrats lost 20 percent among the working class, but lost only 2 percent among the middle class.

The Changing Social Composition of the Democratic Presidential Coalition

The erosion of working-class white loyalties for the Democrats, as well as the massive increase in turnout among blacks, have transformed the social composition of the Democratic presidential coalition (see Table 2-3).[1] Working-class whites made up two-thirds of the Democratic presidential coalition in 1948,[m] but that proportion declined in each subsequent election; by 1972, just over a third of McGovern's votes came from working-class whites. Middle-class whites

---

[1] The percentages in Table 2-3 can be calculated from the data presented in Table 2-1 by converting the percentages to numbers through multiplication, adding up the total number of Democratic voters, and dividing the number of Democratic voters in each sub-group by the total number of Democratic voters. Persons who based these percentages on all Democratic voters, including those excluded from my analysis, will arrive at slightly different results.

Similar results will be obtained using the formula developed by Robert Axelrod for calculating the percentage of votes each sub-group contributed to a party's electoral coalition. (See Axelrod, "Where the Votes Come From.") Axelrod does not examine the behavior of blue-collar workers, although he examines the contribution of nonwhites and of union members to the Democratic coalition.

[m] I have not used the 1944 NORC survey for Table 2-3, for it is based upon a quota sample that overrepresents white-collar workers.

Table 2-3
Social Composition of the Democratic Presidential Coalition from 1948 to 1972[a]

Year of Election:	Working-Class Whites	Middle-Class Whites	Working-Class Blacks	Middle-Class Blacks	Total Percent	(Number)
1948	66%	28%	6%	1%	100%	(154)
1952	58%	33%	7%	2%	100%	(410)
1956	54%	39%	7%	†	100%	(425)
1960	52%	40%	7%	2%	101%	(628)[b]
1964	49%	39%	9%	4%	101%	(653)
1968	40%	41%	14%	5%	100%	(350)
1972	37%	41%	14%	8%	100%	(486)

[a]Not including farmers, permanently unemployed, or persons who are neither white nor black.
[b]Weighted N.
†Less than one percent.

made up just over one-fourth of the Democratic coalition in 1948, one-third in 1952, but, from 1956 on, two out of five Democratic votes came from middle-class whites. By 1968 Humphrey received as many of his votes from middle-class whites as from working-class whites; in 1972 McGovern received more of his votes from the white middle class than from the white working class. The black contribution to the Democratic coalition grew markedly during the postwar years. In 1948 Truman received only one in fourteen of his votes from the black electorate, and even in 1960 Kennedy received less than one in ten of his votes from blacks. In 1964, however, the black contribution jumped to one in seven, both because black turnout increased and because nearly all black voters supported Johnson. Humphrey received nearly one in five of his votes from black voters, and over a fifth of McGovern's support came from blacks.

These data strongly suggest that gaining black votes has been costly to the Democratic coalition. Especially in 1968 and 1972 high levels of black support have been accompanied by massive defections from working-class whites. That these defections were often to Wallace in 1968 further suggests that they were race-related.[28] And, as we will see in Chapter 6, attitudes toward race-related issues strongly influenced voting behavior in 1972. It is by no means inevitable, however, that gaining black votes must cost votes among working-class whites. In 1964 Johnson received massive support from blacks, but he also won three out of four white working-class votes. The possibility of a coalition between working-class whites and blacks, advocated by Jack Newfield and Jeff Greenfield, cannot be dismissed, for these groups may have similar economic interests.[29] Robert Kennedy might have forged such a coalition. But no such coalition emerged in 1968 or 1972.

Simple demography dictates that a national electoral coalition based predominantly upon black votes cannot win, for, as Richard M. Scammon and Ben J. Wattenberg remind us, most voters are "unblack."[30] Therefore, it would be misleading to base projections upon the data in Table 2-3 and conclude that the black contribution to the Democratic presidential coalition will continue to grow. To be successful, the Democrats must regain white support, and Democratic leaders will be tempted to abandon or play down appeals to blacks. These temptations will be reinforced by the assumption that blacks have no viable electoral alternative but to vote Democratic. It is widely assumed that blacks who are dissatisfied with the Democrats can merely abstain (or waste their vote on a third party).[n] Simple arithmetic shows that a vote converted from the opposition party

---

[n]Given the American electoral system, votes for president have no effect unless a candidate receives a plurality in an electoral unit. Unless whites were highly fragmented among several candidates, blacks could command a plurality only in the District of Columbia. Whites who voted for Wallace in 1968 might have affected the result by depriving any candidate of a majority of the electoral vote. Wallace would then have been able to use his electoral votes to bargain with other candidates or to force the election into the House of Representatives. But as a black party is unlikely to be in such a bargaining position, for blacks to vote for a black party would have the same effect as abstaining. Of course, blacks, together with Left of Center whites, could form a third party of the Left that might gain some electoral votes, especially if Center and Right parties were fragmented.

is worth as much as two votes lost to abstentions.[31] Each white vote gained from the Republicans can compensate for two blacks who do not go to the polls. The assumption that blacks have no viable electoral alternative may prove especially costly to them. Black leaders are aware of this problem, and have urged blacks to be more politically independent.[32] But recognizing this problem provides no solution unless the Republicans choose candidates and issues that provide blacks with an alternative.

Some Democratic leaders have already begun to play down their appeals to blacks. Modifying the demographic guidelines, more often called quotas, that guaranteed proportional representation for blacks at the Democratic national convention is one significant step in this direction. Promoting George Wallace into the ranks of honored Democratic leaders is another. Yet, it is by no means certain that the Democrats will abandon their appeals to blacks, for, as we will see in our analysis of attitudinal data, many young college-educated Democrats share the attitudes and feelings of blacks.

Regardless of what policies the Democrats adopt, however, the total black contribution to the Democratic presidential coalition is unlikely to grow. The high black contribution to the Democratic coalition in 1968 and 1972 was caused largely by the low level of Democratic support among whites. If white support for the Democrats increases markedly, the relative contribution of blacks must decline.

But the white middle-class contribution to the Democratic coalition may grow. The white middle class and the white working class are of roughly equal size, but middle-class whites more often vote than working-class whites. Thus, when the relationship of class to party choice is negligible, as in 1972, the Democrats gain more of their total support from the middle class. Our projections suggest that the white middle class will become an increasingly important source of Democratic support. That projection is not based upon a simple analysis of the relationship of social class to party choice over time, but upon a more intensive analysis of that relationship among age groups.

Notes

1. See Frank Parkin, *Class Inequality and Political Order: Social Stratification in Capitalist and Communist Societies* (New York: Praeger, 1971), pp. 116-21.

2. See David Butler and Donald Stokes, *Political Change in Britain: Forces Shaping Electoral Choice*, 2d ed. (New York: St. Martin's, 1974), Chapter 9. Also see, Paul R. Abramson, "Generational Change and Continuity in British Partisan Choice," paper presented at the IXth World Congress of the International Political Science Association, Montreal, Canada, August, 1973.

3. U.S. Bureau of the Census, *Statistical Abstract of the United States:*

1972, 93d ed. (Washington, D.C.: U.S. Government Printing Office, 1972), p. 315.

4. See Gabriel Kolko, *Wealth and Power in America* (New York: Praeger, 1962); Herman P. Miller, *Income Distribution in the United States*, U.S. Bureau of the Census, A 1960 Census Monograph (Washington, D.C.: U.S. Government Printing Office, 1960). For a summary of recent trends, see Christopher Jencks, *Inequality: A Reassessment of the Effect of Family and Schooling in America* (New York: Basic Books, 1972), pp. 209-13.

5. For a summary of the mean incomes of persons in different occupational categories between 1950 and 1970, see *Statistical Abstract*, 1972, p. 328.

6. U.S. Bureau of the Census, *Historical Statistics of the United States: Colonial Times to the Present* (Washington, D.C.: U.S. Government Printing Office, 1960), p. 74.

7. U.S. Department of Labor, *Manpower Report of the President* (Washington, D.C.: U.S. Government Printing Office, 1973), p. 142. These data are not fully comparable with figures from 1900 to 1950, for the earlier figures are based upon persons 14 years and older, whereas the more recent figures are based upon persons 16 years and older. The earlier figures are based upon the "economically active population," including the unemployed, whereas the more recent figures include only those unemployed persons currently available for work who are actively seeking employment. (See Manpower Report of the President, pp. 119-20.)

8. See Daniel Bell, *The Coming of Post-Industrial Society: A Venture in Social Forecasting* (New York: Basic Books, 1973), pp. 123-42.

9. See Frances Fox Piven and Richard A. Cloward, *Regulating the Poor: The Functions of Public Welfare* (New York: Vintage Books, 1971), pp. 200-21.

10. *Statistical Abstracts*, 1972, p. 26 and U.S. Bureau of the Census, *1970 Census of the Population: General Social and Economic Characteristics* (Washington, D.C.: U.S. Government Printing Office, 1972), p. 380.

11. See Angus Campbell, Philip E. Converse, Warren E. Miller, and Donald E. Stokes, *The American Voter* (New York: Wiley, 1960), pp. 351-61.

12. For a discussion of status polarization, see Campbell, et al., *The American Voter*, pp. 344-46.

13. Ibid., pp. 356-67.

14. Ibid., p. 357.

15. Robert R. Alford, *Party and Society: The Anglo-American Democracies* (Chicago: Rand McNally, 1963), pp. 219-49.

16. Ibid., p. 226. Alford provides more recent analysis, which includes results through 1964, in "Class Voting in the Anglo-American Political Systems," in Seymour Martin Lipset and Stein Rokkan, eds., *Party Systems and Voter Alignments: Cross-National Perspectives* (New York: Free Press, 1967), pp. 67-93, at pp. 84-88.

17. See Alford, *Party and Society*, pp. 86-90 and Walter Korpi, "Some

Problems in the Measurement of Class Voting," *American Journal of Sociology*, 78 (November, 1972), 627-42.

18. Alford, *Party and Society*, p. 88.

19. Korpi, "Some Problems," pp. 630-31.

20. See Richard F. Hamilton, *Class and Politics in the United States* (New York: Wiley, 1972), p. 218.

21. Noval D. Glenn, "Class and Party Support in 1972," mimeo.

22. For a discussion of problems with the 1948 Gallup surveys, see Frederick Mosteller, Herbert Hyman, Philip J. McCarthy, Eli S. Marks, and David B. Truman, *The Pre-Election Polls of 1948: Report to the Committee on Analysis of Pre-Election Polls and Forecasts* (New York: Social Science Research Council, 1949), pp. 325-51.

23. See Berelson, Paul F. Lazarsfeld, and William McPhee, *Voting: A Study of Opinion Formation in a Presidential Campaign* (Chicago: University of Chicago Press, 1954), pp. 55-56.

24. See *The Future of American Politics* (Garden City, N.Y.: Doubleday, 1956), pp. 227-34.

25. Hamilton, *Class and Politics*, p. 140.

26. For a more extensive analysis, using the SRC data, of the relationship of social class to voting behavior in the 1952 and 1956 elections, see Heinz Eulau, *Class and Party in the Eisenhower Years: Class Roles and Perspectives in the 1952 and 1956 Elections* (New York: Free Press, 1962).

27. *Class and Politics*, pp. 353-56; 537-41.

28. For a discussion of Wallace's appeals, see Seymour Martin Lipset and Earl Rabb, *The Politics of Unreason: Right-Wing Extremism in America, 1790-1970* (New York: Harper and Row, 1970), pp. 365-427.

29. See Jack Newfield and Jeff Greenfield, *A Populist Manifesto: The Making of a New Majority* (New York: Warner, 1972).

30. See Richard M. Scammon and Ben J. Wattenberg, *The Real Majority* (New York: Coward, McCann, and Georghegan, 1971), pp. 45-58.

31. For a lucid discussion of this point, see Robert Axelrod, "Where the Votes Come From: An Analysis of Electoral Coalitions: 1952-1968," *American Political Science Review*, 66 (March 1972): 19-20.

32. For example, see Chuck Stone, *Black Political Power in America* (Indianapolis: Bobbs-Merrill, 1968), pp. 56-57.

3 Generational Change and the Erosion of Class Voting

Will the relationship between class and party remain low? This question cannot be answered definitively, for as Otis Dudley Duncan reminds us, "There is nothing about a trend—supposing it to have been reliably ascertained for some specific period—that guarantees its own continuation."[1] But one can gain greater confidence about the direction of a trend by studying subgroups that may provide a guide about future relationships.[2] One promising method is to examine age-group differences, for the behavior of the young is more likely to point to future relationships than that of their elders. "It is the inevitable fact of life," Herbert H. Hyman writes, "that the young will replace the old and will determine the future course of any trend. Thus if the young differ from the old, and were to continue to do so despite their own aging, some prediction can be ventured."[3]

This chapter will show that the declining relationship between social class and partisan choice results largely from generational change. Through 1968, strong relationships between class and party persisted among voters who had entered the electorate before or during World War II, but among voters who entered the electorate after the war, these relationships were weak. Increased Democratic voting by the young middle class caused this change. Simple economics do not explain this shift among the young middle class, although it partly results from the differential social composition of the young middle class as compared with its elders. By examining these changes I will strengthen my conclusion that class-based voting is eroding and, more important, will examine a process through which partisan alignments may change.

The authors of *The American Voter* noted age differences in the class-party nexus, and their analysis provides a useful point of departure. To strengthen their interpretation of the declining relationship between class and party choice, they focused on persons who were in their twenties and thirties during the Great Depression. In the 1948 and 1952 presidential elections, status polarization was highest among the "Depression generation." High status polarization among this age group, they suggested, resulted from the economic conditions of the Depression. They acknowledged that "when we deal with age we cannot be sure that patterns that make historical sense are not due instead to the phenomena of the life cycle,"[4] but they did not systematically compare a life-cycle and a generational explanation for their findings.

In the 1956 election, status polarization dropped among every age group, but it fell most among the Depression generation. "It is this portion of the electorate," Campbell and his colleagues write, "that showed the greatest relative depolarization and that best illustrates the fading effects of the Depression."[5] But although age-group differences had all but disappeared, traces remained, and the authors surmised that generational effects may have become latent. They correctly concluded that data covering a longer time span were needed.

Alford, as we saw, objected to Campbell's overall conclusion that the relationship between class and party choice was declining. He also questioned Campbell's conclusions about age-group differences, arguing that whether "age differences at one point in time truly reflect past behavior and the differential impact of a historical crisis is an inference which may or may not be justified."[6] But Alford did not conduct his own systematic analysis of age-group differences.

My analysis of age-group differences over a 24-year period suggests that Campbell and his colleagues correctly concluded that the relationship of class to partisan choice was declining. Their historical interpretation of age-group differences was based upon inference, but my analysis suggests those inferences were correct. The authors of *The American Voter* were premature, however, in judging that generational effects had been eliminated. They overlooked the beginnings of a trend toward much lower levels of status polarization among young voters, a trend that largely accounts for the declining relationship of social class to partisan choice.

Age-Group Differences in Postwar Presidential Elections

Figures 3-1 through 3-7 present the proportion of middle- and working-class major-party voters who supported the Democratic presidential candidate in each election from 1948 through 1972. The data are presented according to age cohorts,[a] and because the Ns for blacks are too small to permit a cohort analysis, I have restricted this analysis to whites.

One can compare similar age cohorts across time by tracing age groups from Figure 3-1 onward, but to facilitate comparison I present two summary measures of the relationship of social class to partisan choice. Levels of class voting for each cohort in each election, as well as the mean level of class voting for the electorate, are presented in Table 3-1. Levels of status polarization for each

---

[a]The term *age cohort* is used to designate any group of persons born during the same time period. The 1952, 1968, and 1972 surveys provided actual data on year of birth (as did the 1970 survey to be analyzed in the following chapters.) For all other surveys, year of birth was calculated from data about the respondent's age.

To maximize comparability over time, the arbitrarily defined 10-year cohorts employed in the 1948 survey were used, even though more detailed data about age were available for subsequent surveys. For persons born after 1923, eight-year cohorts were used. Ideally, four-year cohorts would have been employed since presidential elections are held every four years, but the small Ns precluded this refinement.

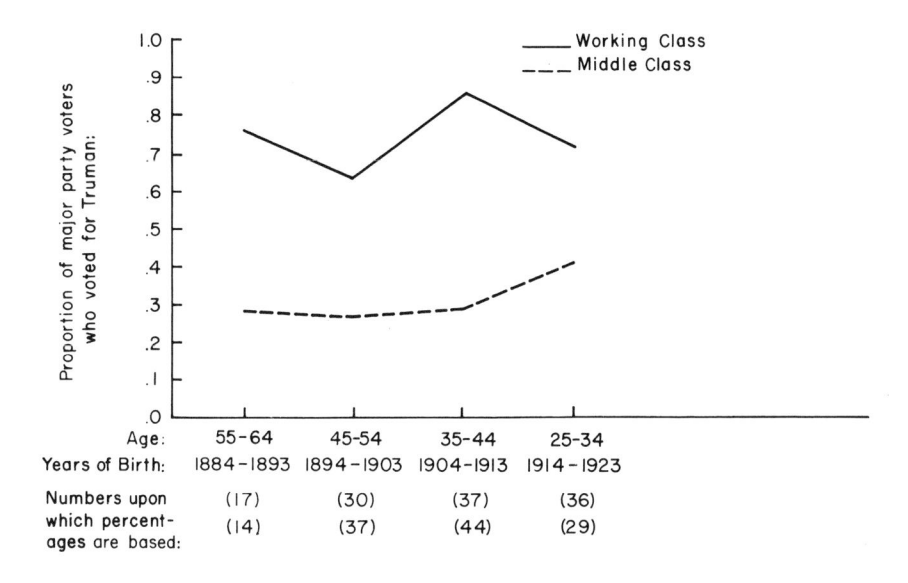

Figure 3-1. Proportion of White Major-Party Voters Who Voted for Truman in 1948, by Social Class and Age

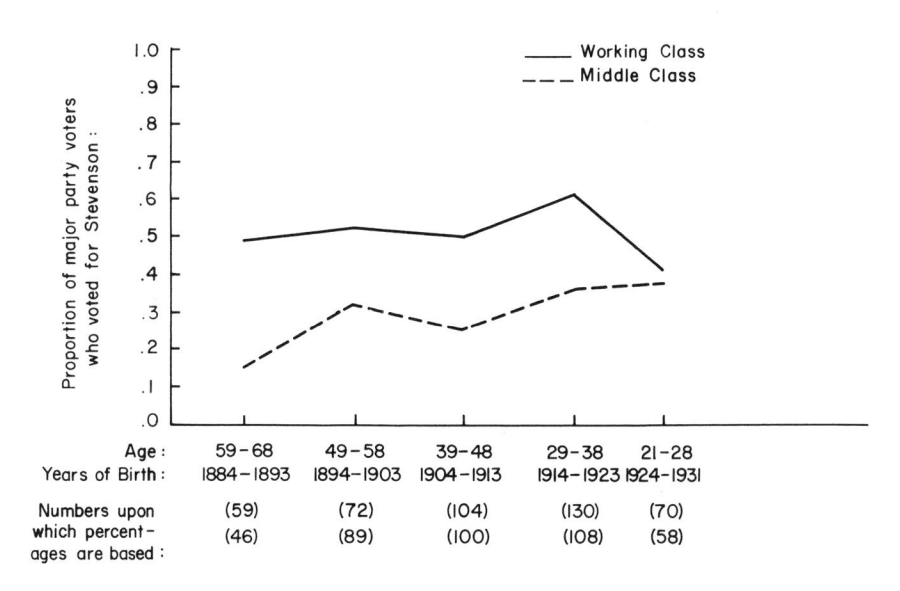

Figure 3-2. Proportion of White Major-Party Voters Who Voted for Stevenson in 1952, by Social Class and Age

[Figure 3-3: graph showing proportion of major party voters who voted for Stevenson, by age and social class]

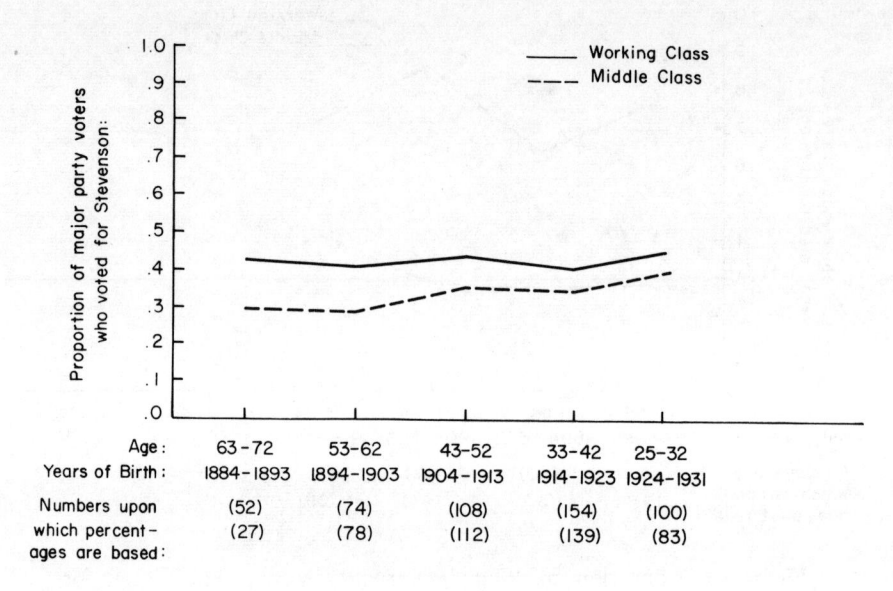

Age:	63-72	53-62	43-52	33-42	25-32
Years of Birth:	1884-1893	1894-1903	1904-1913	1914-1923	1924-1931
Numbers upon which percentages are based:	(52) (27)	(74) (78)	(108) (112)	(154) (139)	(100) (83)

Figure 3-3. Proportion of White Major-Party Voters Who Voted for Stevenson in 1956, by Social Class and Age

[Figure 3-4: graph showing proportion of major party voters who voted for Kennedy, by age and social class]

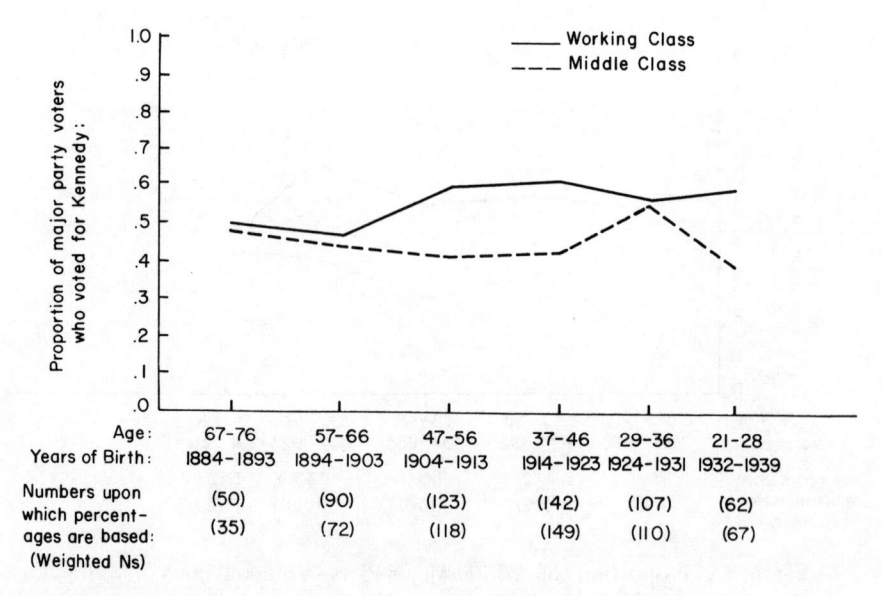

Age:	67-76	57-66	47-56	37-46	29-36	21-28
Years of Birth:	1884-1893	1894-1903	1904-1913	1914-1923	1924-1931	1932-1939
Numbers upon which percentages are based: (Weighted Ns)	(50) (35)	(90) (72)	(123) (118)	(142) (149)	(107) (110)	(62) (67)

Figure 3-4. Proportion of White Major-Party Voters Who Voted for Kennedy in 1960, by Social Class and Age

[Graph: Proportion of major party voters who voted for Johnson, by Age and Social Class]

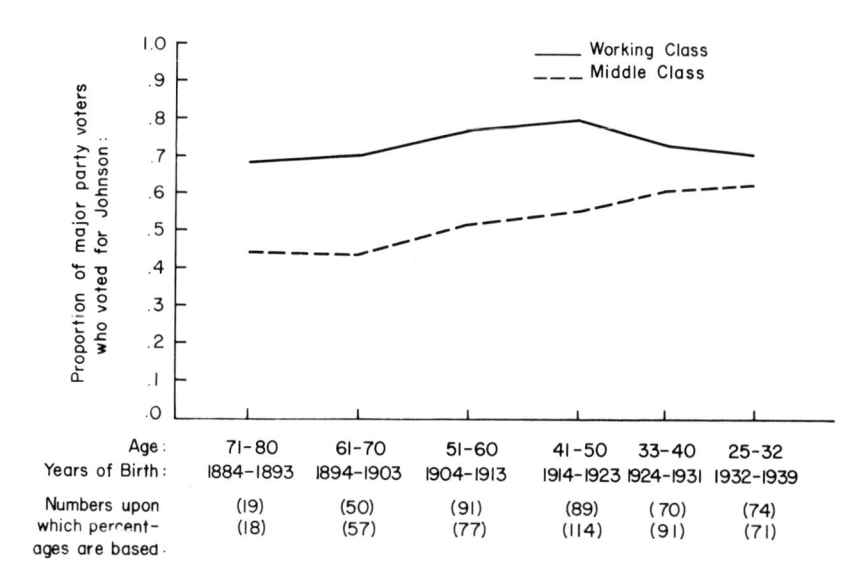

Age:	71-80	61-70	51-60	41-50	33-40	25-32
Years of Birth:	1884-1893	1894-1903	1904-1913	1914-1923	1924-1931	1932-1939
Numbers upon which percentages are based	(19) (18)	(50) (57)	(91) (77)	(89) (114)	(70) (91)	(74) (71)

Figure 3-5. Proportion of White Major-Party Voters Who Voted for Johnson in 1964, by Social Class and Age

[Graph: Proportion of major party voters who voted for Humphrey, by Age and Social Class]

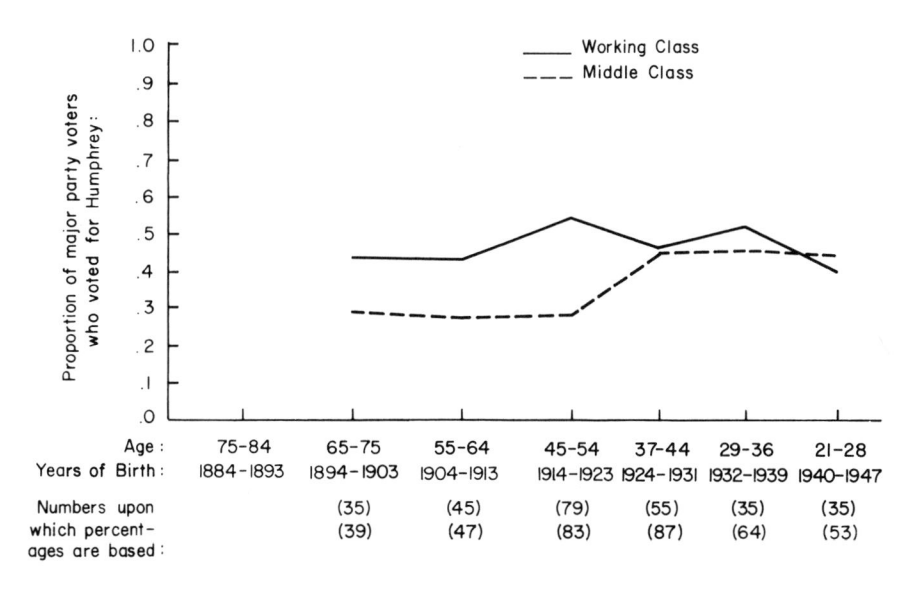

Age:	75-84	65-75	55-64	45-54	37-44	29-36	21-28
Years of Birth:	1884-1893	1894-1903	1904-1913	1914-1923	1924-1931	1932-1939	1940-1947
Numbers upon which percentages are based:		(35) (39)	(45) (47)	(79) (83)	(55) (87)	(35) (64)	(35) (53)

Figure 3-6. Proportion of White Major-Party Voters Who Voted for Humphrey in 1968, by Social Class and Age

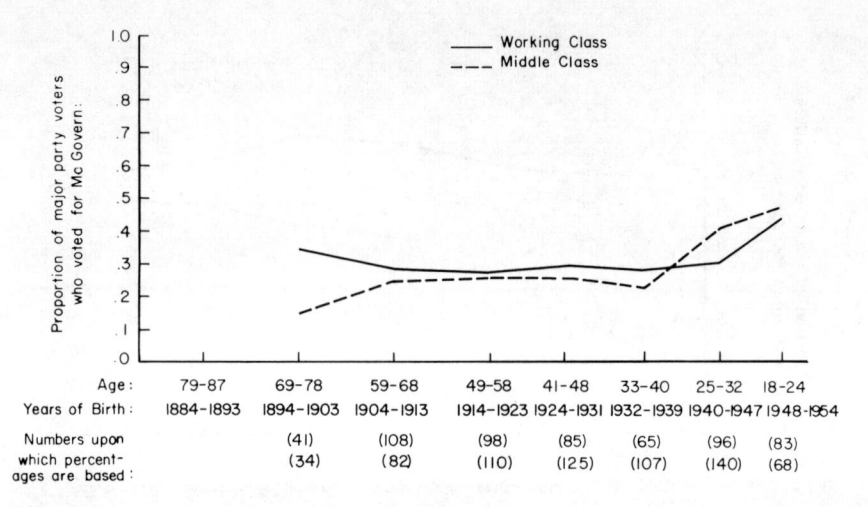

Figure 3-7. Proportion of White Major-Party Voters Who Voted for McGovern in 1972, by Social Class and Age

cohort in each election, as well as the overall level of status polarization for the electorate, are reported in Table 3-2.

Campbell and his colleagues may have concluded prematurely that the effects of the Depression had faded away. The Depression cohort born between 1904 and 1913 had the highest level of class voting and of status polarization in 1948. Although age-group differences were negligible in 1956, that cohort had higher than the mean level of class voting in three of the four subsequent elections. It was the only cohort that never fell below the mean level of class voting in any presidential election (see Table 3-1). Moreover, the 1904-13 cohort was the only age-group that consistently had higher than the mean level of status polarization in all seven elections (see Table 3-2).

But focusing on the distinctive effects of the Depression upon the 1904-13 cohort leads one away from analyzing far more striking age-group differences. In analyzing the 1952 election, Campbell and his colleagues overlooked the marked differences between all older cohorts and the youngest cohort that entered the electorate after World War II. Whereas social class related strongly to partisan choice among the cohorts born before 1924, there was virtually no relationship between class and presidential vote among voters born between 1924 and 1931 (see Figure 3-2, Tables 3-1 and 3-2). Campbell and his colleagues may have felt it prudent to overlook this difference. Their only data point after 1952 was 1956, when cohort differences were negligible. Any age-group difference discovered at only one point in time could result from sampling error. But, more important, the low relationship of social class to partisan choice among young voters could

Table 3-1
Class Voting[a] Among Whites, by Years of Birth in Seven Presidential Elections

Years of Birth:	1884-1893	1894-1903	1904-1913	1914-1923	1924-1931	1932-1939	1940-1947	1948-1954	$\bar{X}$ for Total White Electorate
Year of Election:									
1948	48	36	57	31	†				44
1952	34	20	24	25	4				20
1956	13	12	8	6	5	†			8
1960	1	2	18	19	1	21			12
1964	24	26	25	25	12	8	†		19
1968	†	15	15	27	1	6	-3		10
1972	†	19	4	2	4	5	-11	-4	2

[a]Class voting is the percentage of working-class respondents who voted Democratic minus the percentage of middle-class respondents who voted Democratic. (Among major-party voters.)
†Because of small Ns, the index of class voting has not been presented.

Table 3-2
Status Polarization[a] Among Whites, by Years of Birth in Seven Presidential Elections

Years of Birth:	1884-1893	1894-1903	1904-1913	1914-1923	1924-1931	1932-1939	1940-1947	1948-1954	$\bar{X}$ for Total White Electorate
Year of Election:									
1948	.62	.40	.65	.26	†				.48
1952	.38	.23	.25	.26	.01				.21
1956	.03	.14	.11	.08	.09	†			.10
1960	.11	.13	.20	.12	.01	.28			.12
1964	.35	.26	.24	.30	.19	.05	†		.21
1968	†	.16	.21	.28	.04	.12	−.04		.12
1972	†	.20	.05	−.01	.04	.00	−.14	−.09	−.01

[a]Status polarization is the Kendall's tau-c relationship between a five-fold ordinal measure of occupation as listed in Table 2-2 and direction of presidential vote (among major-party voters).
†Because of small Ns, the level of status polarization has not been presented.

be due to "the phenomena of the life cycle." Indeed it is easy to develop a plausible life-cycle explanation for this relationship.

A life-cycle explanation for this relationship assumes that young persons are less affected by their social class than older persons are because the young have had less experience in the work force than their elders and have had less time to learn the social and political norms of their class. Moreover, many of the young will have recently crossed class lines through intergenerational social mobility. Both upwardly and downwardly mobile individuals may be slow to accept the norms of the class they have entered. A life-cycle explanation suggests that as young persons gain more experience in the work force they will become socialized more fully to the norms of their social class. As this socialization occurs, an increasing proportion will learn to support the prevalent party of their class. The net effect of this socialization (and resocialization) will be an increasing relationship between social class and partisan preferences. If the life-cycle explanation were valid, the low relationship of class to party among the young could not be interpreted as the beginning of a trend, since that relationship would rise in subsequent elections.

But the low relationship between class and party among the young could also be explained by a generational explanation similar to that used (but not fully developed) by Campbell and his colleagues to account for the behavior of the "Depression generation." The young may have had formative experiences different from those of their elders. Whereas their elders may have had formative experiences that contributed to a high relationship between social class and partisan choice, young voters may have had experiences that contributed to a low relationship. Before attempting to discriminate between explanations, we should examine more fully the assumptions that constitute a generational explanation.

A political generation is "a group of persons who have undergone the same basic historical experiences during their formative years."[7] A generational explanation for age-group differences assumes that there is a formative socialization period during which fairly enduring attitudes are learned; after that, attitudes tend to become relatively stable. While such assumptions are not valid for all political attitudes, there is a good deal of evidence that they may be valid for party loyalties.[8] Many persons learn and accept their parents' party preferences. The experiences most likely to change a person's partisan loyalties probably occur between the time he enters the work force and the first few elections in which he participates.[b] During this period a person is most likely to be socially and geographically mobile. Many will marry and further weaken parental ties. Although many persons will have party loyalties even before they vote, they have had few oppor-

---

[b]Some people will have formative socialization experiences later in their lives. Some will experience career mobility from one class to another. The generational explanation assumes that, for most persons, late adolescence and early adulthood will be especially significant in shaping partisan attachments, and that, for many persons, these attitudes will be relatively stable.

tunities to reinforce those loyalties through political behavior. If economic, social, and political conditions contribute to a strong relationship between class and partisanship during this formative period, that relationship will tend to persist. Even if many individuals change their partisan preferences in a given election, the net relationship between class and party for the generation will tend to be high.[c] But if political conditions during this formative period contribute to a weak relationship between class and party, that relationship is likely to remain low.[d]

If the assumptions constituting the generational explanation are correct, most persons between the ages of 21 and 28 in 1952 had their critical socialization experiences during or after World War II. For most, 1952 was their first presidential election,[e] and many would still be relatively open to partisan change. How they would change would depend on their experiences after 1952. A generational explanation would not necessarily predict a rise or a decline in the relationship of social class to partisan choice. But given the absence of class-based politics during the Eisenhower years, one would expect the relationship of class to partisanship to remain relatively low.

The life-cycle and generational explanations thus lead to contrasting predictions about the future relationship between social class and partisanship.[f] If the low relationship of social class to partisanship among the youngest cohort in 1952 resulted from its relatively recent entry into the work force, that relationship would increase as the cohort gained more work experience and as persons became socialized more fully to the norms of their social class. The relatively low relationship of class to party would be temporary, and overall relationships between class and party would continue for the proximate future. But if the low relationship between class and party choice among the young resulted from fundamental differences between their formative socialization and that of their elders, the overall relationship between social class and partisan choice might decline as new cohorts entered the electorate.

---

[c]As is apparent from the data in this chapter, the relationship between class and party for any given cohort will vary from election to election. Even for the Depression cohort, that relationship was weak in 1956 and 1972, when political conditions contributed to a low relationship between class and party.

[d]This does not mean that cohorts that entered the electorate during a period of low class polarization will remain unaffected by conditions that exacerbate class differences. The cohorts born before 1904 entered the electorate when the relationship between class and party may have been weak. Yet, these cohorts have often attained relatively high levels of class voting, although they have not displayed the distinctively high levels of class voting of the Depression generation.

[e]According to recall questions in the 1952 survey, 42 percent of the voters born between 1924 and 1931 voted in 1948. (Among 1952 voters born between 1924 and 1927, 68 percent had voted in 1948.) Even among those who had voted in 1948, class voting in 1952 was only +6. Since the Ns for this subset of 1948 voters are small, one should be cautious in making inferences from this finding. But there is little evidence that voting in 1948 was a formative experience contributing to high levels of class voting among first-time voters in that election.

[f]Under some circumstances these two explanations would lead to similar predictions. In such cases, a time-series cohort analysis could not distinguish between the explanations.

These explanations can be tested by a time-series cohort analysis.[9] Since there are no panel data over a long time span, one cannot compare identical respondents sampled at different times; but each cohort sampled in 1952 can be compared with similar cohorts sampled in subsequent elections. A life-cycle explanation predicts that the relationship of class to party will rise among the 1924-31 cohort as the mean age of that cohort increases; a generational explanation predicts that the relationship will remain relatively low.

Before examining cohorts across time it may be useful to spell out some of the basic assumptions of cohort analysis. Cohort analysis assumes one has a representative sample of each age group. All seven Survey Research Center (SRC) surveys were based upon national random samples. Even when a random sample is used, however, the probability that subgroups represent the universe of people who belong to those subgroups is less than the probability that the total sample reflects the total universe of persons from whom the sample was drawn. On the other hand, when the same relationships occur among a subgroup in numerous surveys based upon separately conducted samples, one can have more confidence that the relationships have not occurred by chance. (It should be noted that more than half the respondents sampled in 1960 were drawn from a panel survey begun in 1956.)

Cohort analysis also assumes that when one traces an age group across time, its social composition is unchanged. (If there is a known change in the social composition of the cohort that is likely to distort the results, one should attempt to compensate for it.) A cohort analysis that traces age groups across time within a geographic region may face severe methodological problems. Migrations between regions may be age-related, and the composition of a cohort within a region may change as a result of these migrations. In the United States, for example, older people often migrate to the South. Thus, a sample conducted in 1972 of persons living in the South who were born, for example, between 1894 and 1903 would not be comparable to a sample of persons born during those same years who lived in the South in 1948. Glenn recognizes that between-region migration poses a problem, but assumes that migration effects will be small. In fact, a more careful cohort analysis would take migration effects into account.[10] Given this difficulty, as well as the small cell sizes that one would obtain if regional analyses were conducted, I focus on nationwide trends.

Tracing the relationship of social class to partisan choice in the five presidential elections since 1952 reveals substantial support for the generational explanation. Although levels of class voting undergo minor fluctuations, class voting among the 1924-31 cohort remains consistently low (see Table 3-1). Except for the 1964 election, status polarization among this cohort has been low (see Table 3-2). Although the mean age of the 1924-31 cohort rose 20 years by 1972, the relationship of social class to partisan choice remained negligible.

The 1932-39 cohort was analyzed first during the 1960 presidential election (see Figure 3-4). The relatively high relationship of social class to partisan choice among this cohort is probably an anomaly.[g] Nevertheless, alternative explanations of partisan change lead to different expectations about the future behavior of that cohort. A life-cycle explanation predicts that the relationship between class and party will rise as the cohort gains more work experience. But given the absence of class-based conflict in the 1960s, a generational explanation predicts that class voting will not rise; indeed, if the young are relatively flexible in their partisan attitudes, the relationship between class and party might decline.

Tracing the relationship of class to partisan choice in three subsequent elections reveals little support for the life-cycle explanation. In 1964, contrary to the predictions of the life-cycle explanation, both class voting (see Table 3-1) and status polarization (see Table 3-2) declined markedly. Class voting among this cohort declined further in 1968, although status polarization rose to the mean level for the electorate. (Including Wallace voters with Nixon voters would reduce class voting to 0, status polarization to .03.) In 1972 class voting was again low, and status polarization was nonexistent.

The youngest cohort sampled in 1968 (see Figure 3-6) presents the only case among 32 comparisons made up through that year in which the middle class voted Democratic more often than the working class did (see Table 3-1). It is the only cohort until then for which status polarization was negative (see Table 3-2). Since Wallace drew disproportionate strength from the young working class, including Wallace voters in the calculations would further reduce both class voting and status polarization; class voting would fall to -7, status polarization to $-.08$.[h] We do not have adequate data to determine whether this reversal prefigures a trend, but the negative relationship between class and party among this cohort persisted in 1972.

In 1972 eighteen-year-olds had been enfranchised, and a large cohort of persons born between 1948 and 1954 entered the electorate. Among this age group, the middle class voted Democratic more than the working class (see Figure 3-7 and Table 3-1) and status polarization was also negative for the higher occupational groups were more likely to vote Democratic than the lower groups (see Table 3-2). In fact, among all five occupational groups of the seven cohorts studied, only voters born after 1947 with professional heads of households gave

---

[g]The low relationship of social class to partisan choice among the two oldest cohorts in 1960 results from high levels of Republican voting among working-class Protestants. But I cannot explain the high relationship of class to party among the youngest cohort.

[h]Norval D. Glenn combined the results of five Gallup surveys conducted shortly after the 1968 election, and his results are based upon Ns substantially larger than those in the SRC survey. He found that among white voters between the ages of 21 and 29, white-collar workers were more likely to vote Democratic than blue-collar workers, a difference that became more pronounced if Wallace voters were included in the analysis. See Glenn, "Class and Party Support in the United States," p. 5.

a majority of their vote to McGovern. Fifty-nine percent of these 27 young voters voted Democratic.[i]

On balance, a longitudinal cohort analysis provides substantial evidence that generational differences account for the low relationship between class and partisan choice among persons who entered the electorate after World War II. The argument that age differences result from differential historical experiences is based upon inference, but such inferences become stronger when patterns appear consistently at many points in time and when alternative explanations can be rejected.

The overall decline in the relationship of social class to partisan choice has occurred largely because an ever-increasing number of voters born after 1923 have entered the electorate.[j] The relationship of class to voting among voters born before 1924 has fluctuated from election to election, but there was only a slight decline between 1952 and 1968. Among voters born before 1924,[k] class voting was +23 in 1952, although it fell to +8 in 1956 and was only +13 in 1960; class voting among this cohort was +24 in 1964 and +20 in 1968 (+16 if Wallace voters are included); in 1972 class voting fell to +6. Status polarization follows a similar trend. Among voters born before 1924, status polarization was .25 in 1952, but dropped to .09 in 1956 and was only .12 in 1960; status polarization among this age group rose to .27 in 1964 and was .22 in 1968 (.17 if Wallace voters are included); in 1972 it fell to .05. Among voters born after 1923, both class voting and status polarization remained low in all six elections. But the proportion of the electorate born after 1923 grew in

---

[i]In his analysis of the 1972 election, Glenn combined the results of five Gallup surveys. He reports that among white voters between the ages of 18 and 29, the working class was more likely to vote Republican than was the middle class. Class voting among this age group was −4. Glenn did not use the five-fold occupational categorization I employed to measure status polarization, but he did examine the relationship of vote to level of education among age groups. He found that college-educated nonsoutherners below the age of 30 made up the only group of whites that gave less than half of its votes to Nixon. I also examined the way people voted controlling for level of education and years of birth. I found that white college graduates born between 1948 and 1954 ($n = 31$) gave 55 percent of their vote to McGovern. Only one other subgroup (among the 34 remaining educational and age groups studied) gave the Democrats a majority of its vote. (Among the 11 white voters with an eighth grade education or less born between 1932 and 1939, six voted for McGovern.)

[j]There is some historical basis for this division. Persons born before 1924 were first eligible to vote before or during World War II; persons born in 1924 and after first entered the electorate after the War. But the generational explanation does not suggest sharp cutoff points between persons born in one year and those born the next, since the age at which formative socialization occurs will vary from individual to individual.

[k]The following analysis includes all persons born before 1924. In an earlier presentation of these data I reported results only for persons born between 1884 and 1923 and the results reported here differ slightly from those I reported earlier. For the earlier analysis, see Paul R. Abramson, "Generational Change in American Electoral Behavior," *American Political Science Review*, 68 (March 1974): 93-105.

each election (from 17 percent in 1952 to 62 percent in 1972) and will continue to grow.

Partisan Change Among the Middle Class

The low relationship of class to party among the postwar electorate mainly results from high levels of Democratic voting among middle-class voters born in 1924 and after. In 1952 the decline in class voting resulted mainly from high levels of support for Eisenhower among the young working class, but in all subsequent elections the prewar[l] and postwar working class differed little in their support for the Democrats. In every election, middle-class voters born in 1924 and after were more likely to vote Democratic than middle-class voters born before 1924.[m] The tendency of the postwar middle-class electorate to vote Democratic appears to be a generational difference, not the transient result of its youth. The relatively high level of Democratic voting among the youngest middle-class cohort in 1952 persisted in each subsequent election except that of 1972 (see Figures 3-2 through 3-7). Although support for Kennedy was low among the youngest middle-class cohort in 1960, that cohort displayed relatively high levels of Democratic voting in 1964 and 1968, though not in 1972 (see Figures 3-4 through 3-7). The youngest middle-class cohort in 1968 provided a relatively high level of support for the Democrats in 1968, and this support persisted in 1972 (see Figures 3-6 and 3-7). The seven-year cohort of middle-class voters that entered the electorate in 1972 was more Democratic than any other group of middle- or working-class voters, and nearly half voted for McGovern (see Figure 3-7).

Let us compare the last three elections. Among major-party voters in 1964, 51 percent of the prewar middle-class electorate voted for Johnson, whereas 62 percent of the postwar middle-class electorate voted Democratic.[n] A simple percentage difference reveals a net advantage of +10 for Johnson among the postwar middle-class electorate. Among major-party voters in 1968, 29 percent of the prewar middle class voted for Humphrey, whereas 41 percent of the postwar middle class voted Democratic. Humphrey thus held a net advantage of +16 among the postwar middle class.[o] Among middle-class major-party voters in 1972, 23 percent of the prewar cohort voted for McGovern, whereas 33 percent of the postwar cohort did. A simple percentage difference reveals a net advantage of +10 for McGovern among the postwar middle class. In 1972, however, the sharpest differences were between middle-class voters born before

---

[l]I refer to persons born before 1924 as the prewar electorate, even though a small proportion entered the electorate during World War II.

[m]Such differences are obvious for 1952, 1956, 1964, 1968, and 1972 merely by inspecting the appropriate figures. Even in 1960, however, the postwar middle class voted slightly more Democratic than the prewar middle class. Data for 1948 also support this trend, but the Ns are too small to be meaningful.

[n]These percentages include persons born between 1940 and 1943 who were not included in Figure 3-5.

[o]The percentage drops to +13 if Wallace voters are included.

1940 and those born in 1940 and after. Among middle-class major-party voters born before 1940, 24 percent voted for McGovern, among those born in 1940 and after, 43 percent did. McGovern thus held a +20 advantage among middle-class voters between the age of 18 and 32 as compared with their elders. A more extensive analysis of middle-class voting behavior in these three elections permits us to test additional explanations for the Democratic preferences of the postwar middle class.

The high levels of Democratic voting among the postwar middle class cannot be explained by its economic circumstances. My analysis of the 1964, 1968, and 1972 surveys shows that in all three years, postwar middle-class voters held higher occupational positions than did prewar middle-class voters. In 1964 the younger middle-class voters had marginally lower family incomes than their elders, but in both 1968 and 1972 the postwar middle class had higher family incomes than older members of the middle class. The Democratic tendencies of the postwar middle-class voters were not caused by perceiving themselves as members of the working class. In all three surveys, members of the postwar middle class were more likely than their elders to identify themselves as middle class. In short, the members of the postwar middle class voted more Democratic than the prewar, even though their economic circumstances, as well as their subjective class identifications, should have tended to make them vote Republican.

The Democratic leanings of the postwar middle class can be explained partly by its political inheritance and its ethnic origins. Given the net movement of persons into the middle class, many persons with working-class Democratic fathers entered the middle class. Moreover, the movement of persons into the middle class has increased markedly among ethnics, because second and third generation Americans have had greater opportunities for advancement than their parents had.[11] Because of these changes, members of the postwar middle class are more likely to have Democratic fathers than their elders. They are also more likely than their elders to be Catholics.[p] As having a Democratic father and being a Catholic both contribute to voting Democratic, the Democratic tendencies of the postwar middle-class voters could result from inherited Democratic loyalties and the political norms and traditions of their religion.

In both 1964 and 1968, controlling for father's party and respondent's religion provided a partial explanation for the Democratic tendencies of the

---

[p]In this analysis, being Catholic provides an indirect measure of having ethnic origins that contributed to voting Democratic. The Survey Research Center surveys for 1964, 1968, and 1972 provide detailed data about ethnic origins. In 1964 and 1968 extensive background data were collected, but there was a tendency for respondents to report themselves as "American only" if both their parents were born in the United States. When ethnic origin was used as a variable, the postwar middle class was only marginally more likely to have Irish, East European, and Southern European origins than was the prewar middle class. In 1972 the SRC measured the respondent's subjective ethnic identification. But younger members of the middle class were only four percent more likely to identify as Irish, East European, or Southern European ethnics than were older members of the middle class.

postwar middle class. In 1964 the tendency of the postwar middle class to vote Democratic more often than its elders was reduced among voters with Republican fathers, and in 1968 the tendency of the postwar middle class to vote Democratic was reduced among respondents with both Republican and Democratic fathers. In all three elections, controlling for respondent's religion reduced the tendency of the postwar middle class to be more Democratic than its elders. Nonetheless, the tendency of the postwar middle class to vote more Democratic than its elders persisted in all three years. In all three years, the tendency of the postwar middle class to be Democratic persisted even when both father's party and respondent's religion were controlled simultaneously.[q]

The tendency of the postwar middle class to vote Democratic seems to go beyond its differing social origins. In part, it reflects attitudinal change. In 1964 postwar middle-class voters supported an active federal government more often than their elders on numerous domestic issues. In 1968 age differences were not as marked, but the young were still more likely to support government activism. Given the comparability of items used in the 1964 and 1968 surveys, I was able to construct an identical index of support for federal government activism for both surveys.[r] This index provides a convenient mechanism for comparing levels of Democratic support among prewar and postwar middle-class respondents while controlling for the more liberal policy preferences of the young.

In both years, but especially in 1964, respondents who supported an active federal government were much more likely to vote Democratic than those opposed to government activism. In both years the tendency of the postwar middle class to vote more Democratic than its elders was reduced once controls for policy preferences were introduced. Nonetheless, the Democratic tendencies of the young persisted, regardless of attitudes toward an active federal government.[s]

The 1972 survey does not contain the items used to build the government activism index,[t] but one component of the index was asked in somewhat different form. Respondents were asked whether the government in Washington should see to it that everyone has a good job and a good standard of living or whether each person should get ahead on his own. Respondents rated their opinion on a seven-point scale, ranging from strong support for government guarantees to strong opposition.[u] Although age differences were not marked,

[q]For a detailed presentation of the data that support these statements for 1964 and 1968, see Abramson, "Generational Change in American Electoral Behavior," 103-104.

[r]The four items used measured support for federal government involvement in aiding education, promoting jobs and prosperity, supporting school integration, and guaranteeing public accommodations for Negroes. (The specific items used were variables 66, 78, 100, and 408 in 1964 and variables 60, 66, 75, and 78 in 1968.)

[s]For a detailed presentation of the data that support these statements, see Abramson, "Generational Change in American Electoral Behavior," 104-105.

[t]Among the four items used to construct this index, only two were repeated in 1972 and they were not available for analysis.

[u]The specific item was variable 172 in the pre-election interview and variable 613 in the post-election interview.

postwar middle-class voters were more likely to favor government guarantees than were their elders. The tendency of the postwar middle class to vote Democratic was reduced somewhat once controls for attitudes toward job guarantees were introduced, but differences still persisted.

In 1972 the main differences among the middle class were between those born before 1940 and those born in 1940 and after, and it is useful to compare these two groups. As persons born in 1940 and after were first eligible to vote after the Eisenhower presidency, we can refer to them as the post-Eisenhower cohort. If we compare members of the post-Eisenhower cohort with their elders (including the postwar cohort born between 1924 and 1939), we find they were slightly more likely than their elders to hold high occupational positions within the middle class, although they had somewhat lower family incomes. These income differences, however, do not account for the marked tendency of the post-Eisenhower middle class to vote for McGovern. Middle-class voters born in 1940 and after did not differ from their elders in their subjective class identifications.

While the post-Eisenhower middle-class voters were not more likely than their elders to have Democratic fathers, they were more likely to be Catholics. When we control for religion, the tendency of the post-Eisenhower middle class to vote Democratic is reduced somewhat, but it persists. The post-Eisenhower middle class was more supportive of job guarantees than its elders, and its tendency to vote for McGovern was reduced somewhat once controls for attitudes toward guarantees were introduced. Nonetheless, the tendency of the post-Eisenhower middle class to vote Democratic persisted, even when these controls were introduced.

My analysis strongly suggests that the younger members of the middle class will continue to vote more Democratic than their elders. This tendency results partly from the social composition of the young middle class, partly from its liberal policy preferences. If new middle-class cohorts continue to provide disproportionate support for the Democrats, and if those in the young working class continue to be no more supportive of the Democratic party than their elders, the relationship between social class and partisan choice will continue to remain low as cohorts less polarized by class make up a continually larger proportion of the electorate.

But the Democratic shift among the young middle class will not necessarily contribute to electoral success. The problem for the Democrats is not merely to do better among postwar middle-class voters than among their elders, but to gain a majority of the vote. Yet, the Democrats have gained a majority of the postwar middle-class voters only in the Johnson landslide of 1964. Even in 1972, when McGovern did markedly better with young middle-class voters than he did among older middle-class voters, he failed to gain a majority of the post-Eisenhower middle class. The Democratic gains among the young middle class tended to reduce anti-Democratic swings in both 1968 and 1972, but they did not provide the basis for Democratic majorities.

Generational Change and the Social Composition of the Democratic Presidential Coalition

Democratic support among the postwar middle class does not provide the basis for Democratic majorities, but it greatly affects the social composition of the Democratic presidential coalition. Table 3-3 shows the social composition of that coalition among the prewar and postwar electorates in the six presidential elections between 1952 and 1972. Among both age groups, the black contribution to the coalition has risen markedly, and by 1972 blacks made up 20 percent of the prewar Democratic voters, 23 percent of the postwar. Among both groups the white working-class contribution has declined, but this decline has been far more pronounced among the postwar electorate. Among the postwar electorate the Democrats received more votes from middle-class whites than from working-class whites in both of the last two elections; among the prewar electorate, the Democrats still receive more votes from working-class whites than from middle-class whites. Among the postwar electorate only a third of the Democratic votes came from working-class whites in 1972; among the prewar electorate, McGovern received nearly half his votes from working-class whites.[v] As the postwar electorate gradually will replace the prewar electorate, the white middle class may become a growing source of votes for the Democratic presidential coalition.

Three factors account for the sizable contribution of the middle-class whites among the postwar electorate. Most important, the postwar middle class has voted substantially more Democratic than its elders. In the last six elections, the postwar middle class has voted nearly as Democratic as the postwar working class, and in 1968 and 1972 there were virtually no class differences among the postwar electorate. Secondly, the postwar electorate is somewhat more middle class than the prewar electorate. In both the last elections, most prewar whites were working class, whereas most postwar whites were middle class. In addition, turnout has been substantially higher among the postwar middle class than among the postwar working class. Turnout has been consistently higher among the middle class than among the working class, as the data presented earlier in Table 2-1 reveal, but these differences usually have been greater among the postwar electorate. As long as class voting remains low among the postwar electorate, the Democrats will continue to receive more of their votes from the postwar middle class than from the postwar working class. If current trends continue, middle-class whites will become an increasingly important component

---

[v]Among the post-Eisenhower cohort in both 1968 and 1972, the Democrats received more of their support from the white middle class than from the white working class. Among the 46 Humphrey voters born in 1940 and after, 30 percent were working-class whites, 50 percent were middle-class whites, 11 percent working-class blacks, and nine percent middle-class blacks. Among the 192 McGovern voters born in 1940 and after, 34 percent were working-class whites, 46 percent middle-class whites, nine percent working-class blacks, and 10 percent middle-class blacks.

Table 3-3
Social Composition of the Democratic Presidential Coalition from 1952 to 1972, by Years of Birth[a]

	Working-Class Whites	Middle-Class Whites	Working-Class Blacks	Middle-Class Blacks	Total Percent	(Number)
Years of Birth:			Before 1924			
Year of Election:						
1952	59%	32%	8%	2%	101%	(354)
1956	54%	40%	5%	1%	100%	(310)
1960	54%	38%	6%	1%	99%	(423)[b]
1964	51%	36%	10%	3%	100%	(376)
1968	50%	32%	13%	5%	100%	(164)
1972	47%	33%	17%	3%	100%	(158)
Years of Birth:			1924 and After			
Year of Election:						
1952	54%	40%	6%	0%	100%	(54)
1956	53%	36%	11%	0%	100%	(108)
1960	48%	43%	7%	2%	100%	(203)[b]
1964	46%	41%	8%	5%	100%	(276)
1968	31%	49%	15%	5%	100%	(185)
1972	33%	44%	12%	11%	100%	(328)

[a]Not including farmers, permanently unemployed, or persons who are neither white nor black.
[b]Weighted N.

of the Democratic presidential coalition as the postwar electorate gradually replaces the prewar.

The findings in this chapter are important, for they provide additional evidence that class voting is declining, and allow us to examine more closely the changing composition of the Democratic presidential coalition. But they are also important because they shed light on one process through which partisan alignments are transformed, namely through generational change in which the relationships between social characteristics and partisan preferences among older generations tend to persist, although older generations gradually are replaced by newer generations among whom different relationships prevail.

Notes

1. Otis Dudley Duncan, "Social Stratification and Mobility: Problems in the Measurement of Trend," in Eleanor B. Sheldon and Wilbert E. Moore, eds., *Indicators of Social Change: Concepts and Measurement* (New York: Russell Sage, 1968), pp. 675-719, at p. 679.

2. See Herbert H. Hyman, *Secondary Analysis of Sample Surveys: Principles, Procedures, and Potentialities* (New York: Wiley, 1972), pp. 223-26.

3. Ibid., p. 243. Duncan also considers the study of age-group differences one of the most promising techniques for predicting trends. See "Social Forecasting—The State of the Art," *The Public Interest*, 17 (Fall 1969), 88-118. Also see, Norman B. Ryder, "The Cohort as a Concept in the Study of Social Change," *American Sociological Review*, 30 (September 1965), 843-61.

4. Angus Campbell, et al., *The American Voter*, (New York: Wiley, 1960), p. 357.

5. Ibid., p. 359.

6. Robert R. Alford, *Party and Society: The Anglo-American Democracies* (Chicago: Rand McNally, 1963), p. 224.

7. Marvin Rintala, "Political Generations," in *International Encyclopedia of the Social Sciences* (New York: Macmillan, 1968), vol. 6, p. 93. Such experiences, as Rintala notes, can create divisions within generations as well as between generations.

8. See Philip E. Converse, "Of Time and Partisan Stability," *Comparative Political Studies*, 2 (July 1969), 139-71; David Butler and Donald Stokes, *Political Change in Britain: Forces Shaping Electoral Choice* (New York: St. Martin's, 1969), pp. 44-64; and Campbell, et al., *The American Voter*, pp. 125-28. Also see, William N. McPhee and Jack Ferguson, "Political Immunization," in McPhee and William Glaser, eds., *Public Opinion and Congressional Elections* (New York: Free Press, 1962), pp. 155-79.

9. For an excellent discussion of the methodology of cohort analysis, see Herbert H. Hyman, *Secondary Analysis*, pp. 274-90. For a more extensive

discussion, see Neal E. Cutler, *The Alternative Effects of Generations and Aging Upon Political Behavior: A Cohort Analysis of American Attitudes Toward Foreign Policy, 1946-1966* (Oak Ridge, Tennessee: Oak Ridge National Laboratory, 1968). Also see, Karen Oppenheim Mason, William M. Mason, H.H. Winsborough, and W. Kenneth Poole, "Some Methodological Issues in Cohort Analysis of Archival Data," *American Sociological Review*, 38 (April 1973), 242-58.

For a cohort analysis that tests the explanations developed in this chapter with British, French, German, and Italian data, see Paul R. Abramson, "Social Class and Political Change in Western Europe: A Cross-National Longitudinal Analysis," *Comparative Political Studies*, 4 (July 1971), 131-55.

10. See, for example, Paul Allen Beck, "Partisan Stability and Change in the American South: 1952-1972," paper presented at the 70th Annual Meeting of the American Political Science Association, Chicago, September, 1974.

11. See Peter M. Blau and Otis Dudley Duncan, *The American Occupational Structure* (New York: Wiley, 1967), pp. 231-38.

4 Generational Change and the Decline of Party Identification

The relationship of social class to presidential voting behavior has declined dramatically during the postwar years. Yet, some would argue that there will be no new partisan alignments until there are changes not only of behavior, but of underlying voter attachments to the political parties. Voters may make, in V.O. Key's words, a "standing decision" to support a party, and that decision may remain unaltered even though they may vote for the opposition in a given election.

Since 1952 the Survey Research Center (SRC) has monitored basic feelings toward the political parties by asking questions that measure partisan loyalties on a continuum, ranging from strong attachment to the Democratic party to strong attachment to the Republicans.[a] The Michigan authors usually classify Independents who lean toward a party as Independents, even though they often behave like weak partisans, because the authors maintain that party identification is a psychological, not a behavioral variable. The concept of party identification, they write, is used to "characterize the individual's affective orientation to an important group-object in his environment."[1] A definition based upon behavior, they argue, "blurs the distinction between a psychological state and its behavioral consequences."[2]

Party identification can be considered an independent variable that explains voting behavior. But one can also study the social characteristics that contribute to the development of party identification, in which case identification becomes the dependent variable. To what extent are working-class respondents more likely to identify as Democrats than middle-class respondents?

To assess the relationship of social class to feelings of party identification, we can use either a dichotomous measure, similar to our measure of class voting, or an ordinal measure of association that treats party identification as a seven-fold continuum. Regardless which measure is used, there has been little change in the relationship of class to party identification during the last two decades. A dichotomous measure based upon persons with strong or weak party identifications (excluding Independents and Independents who lean toward a party) shows class-based partisanship among whites to be +16 in 1952 and

---
[a]Respondents are asked, "Generally speaking, do you usually think of yourself as a Republican, a Democrat, an Independent, or what?" Persons who call themselves Republicans or Democrats are asked, "Would you call yourself a strong (Republican, Democrat) or a not very strong (Republican, Democrat)?" Persons who call themselves Independents are asked, "Do you think of yourself as closer to the Republican or Democratic party?"

+18 two decades later;[b] if Independent leaners are included, class-based partisanship was +14 in 1952 and remained +14 in 1972.[c] A measure of association between occupational ranking and direction of party identification yielded a correlation of .11 in 1952 and an identical correlation in 1972.[d] Moreover, generational differences, though present, were not marked. The prewar-postwar dichotomy, which proved useful in analyzing voting behavior, yields no results when analyzing the relationship of class to party identification. But there is a clear difference between persons born in 1940 and after and those born before 1940. In 1968 there was no relationship between class and party identification among the 1940-47 cohort, only a weak relationship in 1970, and no relationship in 1972; moreover, the 1948-54 cohort showed no relationship between class and party identification in either 1970 or 1972. Put differently, among the cohort that showed a slight negative relationship between class and presidential vote in both 1968 and 1972, there was no relationship between class and party identification. Likewise, the cohort that first voted in 1972, and which also had a weak negative relationship between class and presidential vote, showed no relationship between social class and party identification.

Perhaps the absence of a relationship between class and party identification among persons born in 1940 and after prefigures a trend, but the data are too sketchy to permit any definitive conclusions. There has been a substantial decline in the proportion of the electorate attached to either major party, however, and that decline results largely from generational change.

The Decline of Party Identification Among the White Electorate

Whether or not large numbers of citizens hold strong party loyalties may have important behavioral consequences. Campbell and his colleagues long have argued that high levels of partisan support among mass electorates contribute to the stability of democratic political systems. Persons with strong partisan feelings, they argue, are more likely to participate in politics; they possess a conceptual framework that helps them interpret new and complex issues; and,

---

[b]This measure of class-based partisanship is calculated by subtracting the percentage of middle-class strong and weak party identifiers who identify as Democrats from the percentage of working-class strong and weak party identifiers who identify as Democrats.

[c]This alternative measure is calculated by subtracting the percentage of middle-class party identifiers and Independent leaners who identify with (or lean toward) the Democrats from the percentage of working-class party identifiers or Independent leaners who identify with (or lean toward) the Democrats.

[d]Based upon a Kendall's tau-c relationship between a five-fold ordinal measure of occupational ranking and a seven-fold measure of party identification. (See Table 2-2 for the five-fold measure of occupation.) The greater the tendency for the lower occupational groups to identify as Democratic and the upper occupational groups to identify as Republican, the higher the relationship.

perhaps most important, they are more likely to resist the appeals of new parties and of leaders outside the traditional party system.[3] While some of these conclusions have been challenged in recent years,[4] the development of party identification remains a central research concern.[5] And the erosion of American party loyalties during the past decade concerns not only political scientists, but others interested in the future of American politics.

Table 4-1 presents the party loyalties of whites between 1952 and 1972.[e] A large and growing proportion of Americans claims to be neither Republican nor Democratic. Regardless how we define attachment to a party, the proportion of identifiers has declined markedly since 1964. In all the surveys from 1952 through 1964, the proportion of whites who were strong party identifiers never fell below 35 percent. By 1970 only 27 percent were strong identifiers; by 1972, when the percentage of strong Democrats dropped sharply, strong partisans were only 24 percent of the total. Through 1964 about three out of four whites were either strong or weak identifiers, but this proportion declined in each subsequent election; by 1972 only 62 percent were strong or weak identifiers. The percentage of pure Independents, that is those who leaned toward neither major party, rose from eight percent in 1964 to 13 percent in 1972.

Is the trend toward weakening party attachments likely to continue? Following the procedures used in Chapter 3, we can examine relationships among age groups. By examining the relationship of age to strength of party identification, we replicate a well-established finding—Young persons have weaker partisan attachments than their elders. The problem is to explain that relationship, and, as I am using data originally analyzed by Campbell and his colleagues, I will use their discussion as a point of departure.

Age and Party Identification in the Mid-1950s

The authors of *The American Voter* clearly demonstrated that young persons have weaker partisan attachments than their elders.[6] Combining data collected in seven surveys from 1952 through 1957, they show the percentage of strong party identifiers increased steadily with age; the percentage of Independents (including Independents who leaned toward one of the major parties[f]) decreased. But Campbell and his colleagues not only presented their findings; they also recognized, and attempted to test, alternative explanations for them.

Age differences could result from generational effects, for "age may mark an historical epoch in which the person has matured or undergone some special

---
[e]Although party identification was measured in 1954, the SRC survey for that year used arbitrary age categories, and the survey cannot be used in my time-series cohort analysis.

[f]In this analysis, the Michigan authors did not differentiate between Independents who lean toward a party and those who did not.

Table 4-1
Party Identification Among Whites from 1952 Through 1972

Year of Survey:	1952 (%)	1956 (%)	1958 (%)	1960 (%)	1962 (%)	1964 (%)	1966 (%)	1968 (%)	1970 (%)	1972 (%)
Party Identification:										
Strong Democrat	21	20	26	20	22	24	17	16	17	12
Weak Democrat	25	23	22	25	23	25	27	25	22	25
Independent, Leans Democratic	10	6	7	6	8	9	9	10	11	12
Independent	6	9	8	9	8	8	12	11	13	13
Independent, Leans Republican	7	9	5	7	7	6	8	10	9	11
Weak Republican	14	14	17	14	17	14	16	16	16	14
Strong Republican	14	16	12	17	13	12	11	11	10	11
Other Party	†	†	†	1	†	1	†	†	†	†
Apolitical	2	2	3	1	3	†	1	1	1	1
Total Percent (Number)	99 (1615)	99 (1610)	100 (1638)[a]	101 (1739)[a]	101 (1168)	99 (1394)	101 (1131)	100 (1387)	99 (1395)	99 (2397)
Strong Party Identifiers:	35	36	38	36	35	36	27	27	27	24
Strong and Weak Party Identifiers:	75	73	77	76	75	75	71	68	66	62

[a] Weighted *N*.
† Less than one percent.

variety of experience that has left an imprint on his attitudes and behaviors."[7] On the other hand, differences between age groups could result from the differing position of people in the life cycle, for "age may serve as an index of the length of time that the individual has lived in a specified state or engaged in a specified behavior."[8] "The historical interpretation of our data," they continued, "would suggest that partisan feeling was more intense several decades ago than now. If older persons have more intense party loyalties than younger, it is a reflection of the politics of an earlier American period."[9]

Campbell and his colleagues attempted to discriminate between explanations, and their findings supported a life-cycle explanation. As their test used cross-sectional data, however, they could not examine the political attitudes of persons as they moved through the life cycle. Among persons who remain attached to the same party throughout their life, one cannot distinguish age, length of attachment to a party, or the period in which persons entered the electorate. But for persons who have switched their partisanship, duration of attachment can be distinguished from age and era of maturation. If the life-cycle explanation were valid, Campbell and his colleagues reasoned, the tendency of the old to have stronger partisan loyalties than the young would be eliminated once duration of attachment were controlled. Campbell et al. tested the relationship between age and strength of party loyalties while controlling for the length of time the respondents identified with their party. When length of attachment was held constant, the young had somewhat stronger party attachments than their elders. "This pattern of relationships," they concluded, "fits very well a more general thesis that group identification is a function of the proportion of a person's life he has been associated with the group. The longer a person thinks of himself as belonging to a party, the stronger his sense of loyalty to it will become."[10]

But Campbell's test is scarcely definitive, for few old persons had short-term party attachments, and only the simplest controls were applied.[g] More important, although older persons who had recently acquired their current party attachments were likely to have weak party loyalties, the causality of this relationship could be the opposite of that suggested by the Michigan authors. Rather than weak party identifications resulting from the brief attachment to a party, the brief duration might result from weak partisan loyalties. Indeed, panel data suggest that weak partisans are more likely to convert to another party than strong partisans, and they are more likely to become weak partisans of the opposite party than to become strong partisans of their new party.[11]

Even without panel data, however, one can discriminate between alternative explanations of the relationship of age to strength of partisanship by comparing

---

[g]The basic procedure was to compare persons 44 years or younger with those 45 years or older. But the authors found only 27 persons 45 years old and older who held their current attachments for less than four years, and only 40 who had held their current attachments for between four and seven years.

similar cohorts sampled at different times. Campbell and his colleagues did not find this kind of analysis attractive, for they had collected data over only five years. By combining the results of surveys conducted at different times, they precluded any tentative effort at examining the effects of aging upon young adults who, even over five years, might have developed stronger party attachments. Now, we can examine age groups over two decades.

Age and Party Identification Between 1952 and 1972

Table 4-2 presents the percentage of whites who were strong party identifiers between 1952 and 1972, Table 4-3 the percentage of party identifiers (combining strong and weak identifiers), and Table 4-4 the percentage of pure Independents.[h] The data are presented according to age cohorts.[i] Let us begin by examining the relationship between age and strength of party identification in 1952. The percentage of strong party identifiers was lowest among persons born between 1914 and 1923 (ages 29 through 38), and was next lowest among those born between 1924 and 1931 (ages 21-28) (see Table 4-2); these 21- to 28-year-olds also had the lowest percentage of strong and weak identifiers (see Table 4-3). Only a small percentage were pure Independents, and there was no relationship between age and being a pure Independent (see Table 4-4). As Campbell's discussion suggests, there are two plausible explanations for the weakness of party loyalties among these young adults. A life-cycle explanation suggests that their weak partisan loyalties result from their political inexperience, whereas a generational explanation suggests that differences exist between the formative socialization of these young adults and that of their elders.

If a life-cycle explanation for the weak party loyalties of the young were valid, their feelings of party identification should grow stronger as they aged. The cohort born between 1914 and 1923, which had the largest percentage of weak partisans, should develop stronger partisanship as it aged. So, too, the cohort born between 1924 and 1931 should develop stronger partisanship as persons in that age group gain more experience and more opportunities to grow attached to the party of their choice; this cohort had the largest percentage of Independents who leaned toward one of the major parties and

---

[h]I am following the procedures used by the Michigan authors by "folding" the party identification measure to combine strong partisans and to combine strong and weak partisans.

[i]With all these surveys, year of birth or actual age was recorded, and one can use any cohort divisions. To maintain comparability with the analysis in Chapter 3, I continued to use the same cohort divisions employed in that chapter. However, I also conducted this analysis dividing persons born before 1924 into eight-year cohorts. The alternative procedure yields similar results, although the consistency in levels of identification from survey to survey among older cohorts is reduced somewhat when smaller cohorts are used.

Table 4-2
Percentage of Whites Who Were Strong Party Identifiers from 1952 Through 1972, by Years of Birth[a]

Years of Birth:	1884-1893	1894-1903	1904-1913	1914-1923	1924-1931	1932-1939	1940-1947	1948-1954	$\bar{X}$ for Total White Electorate
Year of Survey:									
1952	43% (193)[b]	43% (267)	34% (342)	24% (395)	30% (249)				35%
1956	48% (157)	40% (225)	36% (313)	33% (435)	27% (293)	28% (98)			36%
1958[c]	47% (155)	43% (236)	35% (316)	36% (419)	32% (275)	31% (155)			38%
1960[c]	43% (162)	43% (239)	35% (341)	32% (435)	34% (307)	34% (194)			36%
1962	50% (94)	47% (157)	42% (212)	30% (257)	30% (194)	21% (183)	†		35%
1964	50% (96)	46% (177)	42% (243)	34% (299)	32% (220)	28% (229)	25% (104)		36%
1966	44% (73)	38% (148)	32% (169)	26% (239)	23% (195)	19% (156)	17% (138)		27%
1968	44% (68)	44% (163)	36% (204)	22% (283)	26% (240)	22% (189)	11% (225)		27%
1970	44% (52)	36% (142)	33% (216)	32% (226)	23% (199)	19% (186)	21% (236)	18% (124)	27%
1972	41% (68)	42% (195)	33% (344)	29% (366)	24% (330)	15% (313)	14% (420)	12% (342)	24%

[a] Percentage who are strong Democrats or strong Republicans.
[b] Numbers in parentheses are the totals upon which percentages are based.
[c] Weighted Ns.
† Because of the small Ns, the percentage of strong partisans has not been presented.

Table 4-3
Percentage of Whites Who Were Strong or Weak Party Identifiers from 1952 Through 1972, by Years of Birth[a]

Years of Birth:	1884-1893	1894-1903	1904-1913	1914-1923	1924-1931	1932-1939	1940-1947	1948-1954	$\bar{X}$ for Total White Electorate
Year of Survey:									
1952	77%[b]	81%	75%	72%	68%				75%
1956	82%	71%	77%	73%	68%	55%			73%
1958	83%	79%	81%	78%	69%	70%			77%
1960	81%	82%	76%	72%	72%	74%			76%
1962	84%	83%	81%	75%	67%	65%	†		75%
1964	83%	84%	81%	74%	71%	69%	65%		75%
1966	81%	77%	75%	72%	67%	67%	59%		71%
1968	91%	78%	75%	71%	66%	67%	44%		68%
1970	87%	73%	77%	73%	62%	61%	55%	48%	66%
1972	85%	80%	73%	73%	65%	56%	49%	45%	62%

[a]Percentage who are strong Democrats, weak Democrats, strong Republicans, or weak Republicans.
[b]For the totals upon which these percentages are based, see Table 4-2.
†Because of the small Ns, the percentage of strong and weak partisan identifiers has not been presented.

Table 4-4
Percentage of Whites Who Were Independents with No Party Leanings from 1952 Through 1972, by Years of Birth[a]

Years of Birth:	1884-1893	1894-1903	1904-1913	1914-1923	1924-1931	1932-1939	1940-1947	1948-1954	$\bar{X}$ for Total White Electorate
Year of Survey:									
1952	8%[b]	4%	7%	6%	6%				6%
1956	6%	12%	8%	9%	9%	13%			9%
1958	5%	6%	9%	5%	9%	12%			8%
1960	11%	5%	12%	9%	7%	12%			9%
1962	4%	5%	5%	9%	14%	8%	†		8%
1964	5%	8%	6%	8%	7%	10%	12%		8%
1966	10%	11%	11%	13%	9%	13%	15%		12%
1968	3%	9%	11%	11%	12%	10%	18%		11%
1970	10%	9%	12%	11%	13%	14%	14%	22%	13%
1972	3%	7%	9%	9%	13%	17%	17%	19%	13%

[a]Percentage of Independents who lean toward neither the Democratic nor Republican party.
[b]For the totals upon which these percentages are based, see Table 4-2.
†Because of the small Ns, the percentage of pure Independents has not been presented.

many of them might become loyal partisans as they aged. Even pure Independents might develop partisan attachments.[j] Thus the percentage of strong and weak party identifiers among the 1924 to 1931 cohort should grow during the subsequent two decades.

A generational explanation is based upon different assumptions and predicts different relationships. The basic assumption, which we discussed in Chapter 3, is that there is a formative socialization period during which fairly enduring attitudes are learned; after that, attitudes tend to become relatively stable. We argued that the most important experiences in changing a person's party loyalties probably occur between the time he enters the work force and the first few elections in which he participates. If social and political conditions contribute to the formation of strong party loyalties during this period, the relative level of partisan identification among the cohort will continue to be high. But if conditions during this formative period contribute to the development of weak party loyalties, party loyalties are likely to remain weak.

If the assumptions that constitute the generational explanation are correct, most persons in the 1914 to 1923 cohort had their formative socialization experiences during the 1930s and World War II, and by 1952 would be relatively resistant to partisan change. Low levels of partisan identification among this cohort might well continue as they aged. Persons born between 1924 and 1931 had their formative socialization experiences during or after World War II, and in 1952 many would still be relatively open to partisan change. A generational explanation would not necessarily predict either a rise or decline in levels of partisan identification. But, given the political and social conditions following 1952, party loyalties might remain low. Party leadership was weak.[12] The division of party responsibility between the president and Congress for much of this period may have dampened the development of strong party loyalties. Candidates, especially Republicans, played down their party and ran highly individualized campaigns. Television, by stressing candidates at the expense of parties, may have further weakened party loyalties. And, although there was rapid social change, neither party seemed capable of capitalizing upon that change by offering programs to reinforce party loyalties. Given these conditions, it is plausible that, in spite of the expectations of the life-cycle explanation, party loyalties might fail to develop among the young as they gained more political experience.

These explanations can be tested by a time-series cohort analysis.[k] A

---

[j]On the other hand, Independence might be a form of loyalty in and of itself. Pure Independents might become more committed to Independence as they gained greater political experience.

[k]All these surveys are based upon national random samples, and as the Ns have been reported, the reader can evaluate the probability that the differences between age groups are likely to result from sampling error. (As weighted Ns were used for 1958 and 1960, tests of significance are not valid for those years.) However, the best assurance that differences between cohorts are meaningful is the replication of age differences in numerous surveys

life-cycle explanation predicts that the overall level of party identification will increase among the 1914 to 1923 and 1924 to 1931 cohorts as their mean age increases; a generational explanation predicts that the overall level of party identification should remain low. To the extent that the youngest cohorts are still relatively flexible in their partisan loyalties, the level of party identification might, indeed, decline.

By tracing cohorts over the next two decades, we find virtually no support for the life-cycle explanation. The percentage of strong partisans among the 1914 to 1923 cohort increased by 1956, but after 1964 it declined; in 1972 the percentage of strong partisans was only five percent greater than it had been two decades earlier (see Table 4-2). The percentage of strong party identifiers among the 1924 to 1931 cohort increased slightly by 1960, but after 1964 the percentage of strong partisans among this age group remained consistently *below* the level achieved in 1952. The 1932 to 1939 cohort attained its highest level of identification in 1960, when it was between the ages of 21 and 28,[1] but the percentage of strong identifiers fell thereafter, and by 1972 it was markedly less than it had been when that cohort first entered the electorate. In 1964, when adult members of the 1940 to 1947 cohort were between the ages of 21 and 24, a fourth were strong partisans; by 1966 this percentage dropped and in 1972 only one in seven was a strong partisan. The youngest cohort sampled in 1970, which included 18-, 19-, and 20-year-olds who had not yet been enfranchised, had the lowest percentage of strong party identifiers. By 1972 the proportion of strong identifiers among this age group had declined to only one person in eight. Among the entire cohort born in 1940 and after, which entered the electorate after Eisenhower's presidency, only 13 percent were strong partisans. Among the entire postwar electorate born in 1924 and after, only 16 percent were. While the very low level of strong identifiers might result partly from the special circumstances of the 1972 election, this analysis provides virtually no evidence that the proportion of strong partisans rises as cohorts age.

The data in Table 4-3 offer no support for a life-cycle explanation. The 1924 to 1931 cohort had the lowest percentage of party identifiers in 1952. That percentage increased marginally by 1964, but declined after that, and by 1972

based upon separately conducted samples. In this respect, too, the data for 1958 and 1960 are less satisfactory, for over half the persons interviewed in those years originally were sampled as part of a panel study begun in 1956. Thus, the consistency in levels of identification in 1956, 1958, and 1960 partly results from sampling procedures.

One can also gain greater confidence that age-group differences are meaningful by replicating this analysis with other data sets. To this end, I report upon a study by Norval D. Glenn who used Gallup data to conduct a similar analysis.

[1]Although I report levels of partisanship among the 1932 to 1939 cohort in 1956 and 1958, the full eight-year cohort was not sampled until 1960. Likewise, the full eight-year cohort born between 1940 and 1947 was not sampled until 1968. In 1970 the SRC began to sample 18-, 19-, and 20-year-olds. The 1948 to 1954 cohort sampled in 1970 includes persons born during a five-year period, and in 1972 includes persons born during a seven-year period.

the percentage of identifiers was somewhat lower than it had been when that cohort first entered the electorate. A relatively small number of persons in the 1932 to 1939 cohort were sampled in 1956, and they had a much lower percentage of identifiers than their elders. This percentage increased by 1958, and reached its highest level in 1960. The proportion declined after 1964, and by 1972 the percentage of identifiers reverted to the 1956 identification level. In 1964 nearly two out of three persons in the 1940 to 1947 cohort were party identifiers; after that this proportion declined, and by 1972 just less than half were. The youngest cohort sampled in 1970 was the only age group in that year among which less than half were identifiers; the percentage declined marginally by 1972. By 1972, among the entire post-Eisenhower cohort, less than half were party identifiers, and among the entire postwar cohort only 53 percent were.

The changing percentage of pure Independents (see Table 4-4) has not been as dramatic, but there is no evidence that persons become less Independent as they age. In 1952 the 1924 to 1931 cohort did not differ from its elders, but the proportion of Independents among this age group increased over a 20-year period such that by 1972 the percentage was twice that of 1952. The 1932 to 1939 cohort, when first sampled in 1956, had the largest percentage of pure Independents of any age group. That percentage fluctuated from survey to survey, but by 1972 it was somewhat higher than it had been 16 years earlier. The 1940 to 1947 cohort, when first sampled in 1964, had the highest percentage of Independents of any age group, and that percentage rose five percent during the next eight years. And the 1948 to 1954 cohort, when sampled in 1970, was the first age group in which over one person in five was a pure Independent, although that proportion dropped to just under one in five in 1972. By 1972, among the entire post-Eisenhower cohort, some 18 percent were pure Independents; among the entire postwar electorate, some 17 percent were.

This analysis strongly suggests that the weak party identifications among the young result from fundamental differences between their socialization and that of their elders. It provides virtually no evidence that the low level of identification among the young is a temporary phenomenon that will change as they age. Moreover, two additional analyses, based upon totally independent data sets, also convincingly refute the life-cycle explanation.

One study includes Norval D. Glenn's and Ted Hefner's excellent cohort analysis of Gallup data collected from 1945 through 1969, and Glenn's updated analysis of surveys conducted in 1971.[13,m] As the Gallup surveys do not distinguish between strong and weak partisans, or between Independents who

---

[m]In these analyses, Glenn employed a weighting procedure to compensate for the tendency of cohorts to become increasingly feminine as they aged. As he reports, sex differences in levels of party identification were small, and his weighting procedures had little effect on his results. In my own analysis, I consistently controlled for sex, but as sex differences were small I did not use a weighting factor to compensate for the tendency of women to outlive men.

lean toward a party and those who do not,[n] these data are roughly comparable to my analysis of the proportion who are strong or weak partisans.[o] Glenn reported a decline in party identification over the 26-year period, from 78 percent in 1945 to 70 percent in 1971, almost all of which occurred after 1965. Glenn's analysis provided virtually no evidence that young adults become more partisan as they age. Based upon their analyses, Glenn and Hefner concluded that "the widely cited finding of Campbell, Converse, Miller, and Stokes that older people have stronger party identification on the average than young adults reflects, largely or entirely, an intercohort rather than a life-stage difference."[14]

In addition to Glenn's analyses, a panel study by M. Kent Jennings and Richard G. Niemi demonstrates conclusively that in recent years young adults have not become more partisan as they aged.[15] In 1965 Jennings and Niemi began with a sample of high school seniors and a sample of their parents; the second wave of their study was carried out early in 1973, and over 1,100 youths and 1,100 parents were interviewed in both waves.[p] In 1965, 25 percent of the youths had been strong party identifiers; by 1973 only 13 percent were. In 1965, 65 percent were strong or weak identifiers; by 1973, 51 percent were. Even the percentage of pure Independents rose slightly, from 13 percent in 1965 to 16 percent in 1973.

These changes, Jennings and Niemi concluded, were "startling." Because a life-cycle explanation clearly would lead us to expect the proportion of identifiers to rise among a cohort that had matured from its late teens into its mid-twenties, the decline of partisan identification, they concluded, "provides a compelling argument for a generation effects interpretation."[16] They then speculated that, "Although there may be a decline in the proportion of Independents [including Independents who lean toward one of the major parties] in the future, it seems likely that the rate of decline will not bring this proportion down to levels observed in previous generations for some years, if ever."[17]

Both the Glenn and the Jennings and Niemi studies lead us to reject a life-cycle explanation for the low level of partisan identification among the young. Both studies support my conclusion that the low level of identification among the young results from generational differences. But none of these authors adequately emphasizes that the *overall* decline in the proportion of identifiers during the postwar years results largely from new persons entering the electorate. Yet, a close inspection of both my results and theirs shows that the

---

[n]Since 1940 the Gallup surveys have asked, "In politics, as of today, do you consider yourself a Republican, Democrat, or Independent?"

[o]Glenn usually reports a slightly higher proportion of identifiers than I discovered using the Michigan data. Glenn's analyses include nonwhites, but this difference does not account for his tendency to find a larger proportion of identifiers than I did. When I include blacks, the overall percentage of party identifiers is affected only marginally.

[p]Although Jennings and Niemi have panel data, they present only total distributions for each sample.

proportion of party identifiers has declined very little among older persons. With few exceptions, the older cohorts have been relatively stable in their levels of partisanship (see Tables 4-2 through 4-4).[q] Moreover, the overall level of party identification among the entire prewar electorate has changed very little.

Among whites born before 1924, 36 percent were strong partisans in 1952, and by 1964, 41 percent were; after 1964 the percentage dropped, and in 1972, 34 percent were strong party identifiers.[r] While the overall proportion of strong partisans had declined 12 percent between 1952 and 1972, the percentage of strong party identifiers among the prewar electorate dropped a mere two percent. The overall decline resulted almost totally from the ever-increasing number of persons who entered the electorate after World War II. The percentage of strong and weak party identifiers among the prewar electorate has remained even more constant. In 1972, 76 percent of the prewar whites were party identifiers; the proportion rose to 80 percent in 1958, and remained at that level in 1964; by 1972 it had declined to 75 percent. While the proportion of party identifiers among the entire electorate declined 13 percent during the postwar years, the proportion among the prewar electorate declined a negligible one percent. Again, the overall decline came from cohorts born after 1923. The proportion of pure Independents among the prewar electorate was only six percent in 1952, and reached 12 percent in 1966; by 1972 it had dropped to eight percent. Among the entire white electorate, the proportion of pure Independents rose seven percent during the two decades studied, but among the prewar electorate, it rose only two percent. Once again, the overall change largely resulted from persons who had entered the electorate after World War II.

Glenn's cohort divisions allow us to approximate closely the prewar, postwar dichotomy.[s] Among persons born before 1925, 78 percent were party identifiers in 1945, and that percentage was unchanged 26 years later. The percentage of party identifiers among the entire electorate had dropped eight percent, entirely as a result of persons born after 1924 entering the electorate. Jennings and Niemi do not present data on the overall decline of party identification among the electorate, but their data show considerable stability in the identifications of the parental generation. In 1965, 34 percent of the parents were strong partisans; in 1973, 30 percent were. In their first wave, 73 percent were strong

---

[q]As I report above, these results are somewhat less stable when persons born before 1924 are divided into eight-year cohorts.

[r]These figures include persons born before 1884.

The changes between 1952 and 1972 partly result from the changing composition of the prewar cohort. The cohorts born before 1894, who had high levels of identification, had higher death rates than the younger prewar cohorts. These older cohorts made up 25 percent of the prewar electorate in 1952, but only eight percent in 1972.

[s]Glenn reports the ages of his cohorts during the year they were surveyed. My reports about the year of birth of his cohorts are based upon my approximations.

As all persons sampled in 1945 were born before 1925, I reported the overall level of identification for that year; with the 1971 data I reported the partisanship of persons born between 1885 and 1924.

or weak identifiers, in the second, 75 percent were. Ten percent were pure Independents in 1965, as was an identical proportion eight years later.

The relative stability of partisan predispositions among older respondents accounts for the importance of generational change. If partisan loyalties were highly malleable, older cohorts would be influenced by the same forces that have impeded the development of strong party loyalties among new cohorts. Generational change is most likely to be an important process in explaining attitudes and predispositions that are relatively stable. Yet, even among older persons partisan loyalties can change. To demonstrate this fact, we could turn to cross-national comparisons and examine countries where partisan change has been far more dramatic than in America.[18] But no cross-national comparisons are needed to demonstrate this point, for one need only examine the partisan loyalties of black Americans.

Party Identification Among Blacks

Table 4-5 presents the partisan identifications of blacks between 1952 and 1972. Among blacks, as among whites, partisan loyalties have weakened in recent years, for there has been a 20 percent drop in the percentage of strong Democrats between 1968 and 1972. Moreover, when we examine the partisanship of blacks over the last two decades we find other sudden changes. Through 1962, about one black in seven was a Republican; in 1964, with Goldwater's nomination, the proportion of black Republicans dropped to one in 14. Through 1962, about one black in seven was classified as "apolitical," that is to say, someone who could not relate himself to the questions used to measure party identification. In 1964, presumably because of the controversies surrounding the Civil Rights Act, as well as efforts by civil rights leaders to mobilize southern blacks, the proportion of apoliticals suddenly dropped to less than one in 20, and remained less than one in 20 in all four subsequent surveys.[19] Such sudden shifts cannot result from generational change, but are caused by political conditions affecting persons of all ages. This fact can be demonstrated by a cohort analysis, but because the number of blacks sampled is small, we must use more broadly defined cohorts than in our analysis of whites.

Table 4-6 presents the percentage of strong and weak Republicans among blacks born before 1914 and among blacks born in 1914 and after.[t] Blacks born

---

[t]Whereas a prewar-postwar cohort dichotomy often has proved useful in analyzing change among whites, a different cohort division was used to examine change among blacks. Blacks have had fundamentally different political experiences, and cohort divisions that are meaningful for whites may not be meaningful for blacks. This is suggested by Donald R. Matthews and James W. Prothro who found that the relationship between age and political participation usually found among whites was not present among blacks. They found that among southern whites, participation increased with age (except for whites 80 and above), whereas among southern blacks participation was highest among those between the ages of 40 and 49. They interpret this difference by arguing that specific generational effects account for high levels of participation among blacks who were in their twenties and thirties when the Supreme Court ruled the white primary unconstitutional. See *Negroes and the New Southern Politics* (New York: Harcourt, Brace, and World, 1966), pp. 71-72.

Table 4.5
Party Identification Among Blacks from 1952 Through 1972

Year of Survey:	1952 (%)	1956 (%)	1958 (%)	1960 (%)	1962 (%)	1964 (%)	1966 (%)	1968 (%)	1970 (%)	1972 (%)
Party Identification:										
Strong Democrat	30	27	32	25	35	52	30	56	41	36
Weak Democrat	22	23	19	19	25	22	31	29	34	31
Independent, Leans Democratic	10	5	7	7	4	8	11	7	7	8
Independent	4	7	4	16	6	6	14	3	12	12
Independent, Leans Republican	4	1	4	4	2	1	2	1	1	3
Weak Republican	8	12	11	9	7	5	7	1	4	4
Strong Republican	5	7	7	7	6	2	2	1	0	4
Other Party	1	1	0	0	1	0	0	0	0	†
Apolitical	17	18	16	14	15	4	3	3	1	2
Total Percent	101	101	100	101	101	100	100	101	100	100
(Number)	(171)	(146)	(161)[a]	(171)[a]	(110)	(156)	(132)	(149)	(157)	(267)
Strong Party Identifiers:	35	34	39	32	41	54	32	57	41	40
Strong and Weak Party Identifiers:	65	68	69	59	73	81	70	87	79	75

[a]Weighted N.
†Less than one percent.

before 1914 entered the electorate no later than 1934 (although if they lived in the South they probably were not able to vote). Those born in 1914 and after entered the electorate either during a period when Roosevelt rapidly was winning the loyalties of black voters or during a period when the Democrats already had won the loyalties of most blacks. Through 1962, older blacks tended to be Republican more often than younger blacks.[u] Presumably this difference reflects the residual Republican loyalties that had developed before the New Deal, although even older blacks were about twice as likely to be Democrats as to be Republicans. But in 1964 the Republicanism among older blacks virtually disappeared. Likewise, the proportion of apoliticals declined among blacks of all ages, and by 1966 older blacks were no more likely to be apolitical than younger blacks.

The rapid change in party identification among older blacks demonstrates that even mature adults may discard established loyalties.[v] In spite of the recent erosion of party loyalties following the Watergate revelations,[w] the long-term decline in party loyalties among whites largely resulted from generational change. Although the current low level of party loyalties may be temporary, we have no basis for projecting that levels of party loyalty will return to those of the late 1950s and the mid-1960s. Rather, there are likely to be few strong partisans and many Americans who identify with neither political party.

Concluding Comments

Although this analysis provided no support for the life-cycle explanation for the weak party loyalties of young adults, that explanation may have been valid for

---

[u]The 1958 survey provides the only exception to this generalization.

[v]Although these rapid changes in party loyalties demonstrate that partisanship can change even among mature adults, blacks are atypical because their party loyalties seldom were reinforced by political behavior. In the South, blacks often were disfranchised and thus had no opportunity to reinforce whatever party loyalties they may have had, and even in the North, blacks participated less often than whites. Thus, even those blacks who claimed to identify with a party may have had weaker party loyalties than their answers to the party identification questions might indicate. This is suggested by Converse who found that southern blacks sampled in a panel survey conducted in 1956 and 1960 often switched their party loyalties over this period. (See "On the Possibility of Major Political Realignment in the South," in Campbell, et al., *Elections and the Political Order*, pp. 212-42, at pp. 233-35.)

[w]In late 1973 and early 1974 party identification levels reached all-time lows. A survey conducted by the University of Michigan Center for Political Studies in October and November of 1973 found that the proportion of party identifiers had declined six percent from the already low levels of late 1972. (See *ISR Newsletter*, 1 [Winter 1974], 6.) The Gallup polls also report a decline in party identification. In the period between June and October 1972, 71 percent were identifiers; during September 1973 through January 1974, 66 percent were. (See *The Gallup Opinion Index*, 105 [March 1974], 22.) Although no detailed analyses were reported, a sudden decline in partisanship during a single year cannot result from generational change alone, for the demographic composition of the electorate changes little during that time.

Table 4-6
Percentage of Blacks Who Identified as Strong or Weak Republicans from 1952 Through 1972, by Years of Birth

Years of Birth:	Before 1914	1914 and After
Year of Survey:		
1952	16% (92)[a]	9% (77)
1956	21% (62)	17% (83)
1958[b]	17% (70)	18% (91)
1960[b]	25% (72)	9% (99)
1962	26% (47)	5% (62)
1964	6% (52)	8% (103)
1966	19% (37)	5% (92)
1968	4% (45)	1% (103)
1970	3% (35)	3% (118)
1972	10% (52)	7% (210)

[a]Numbers in parentheses are the totals upon which percentages are based.
[b]Weighted Ns.

earlier periods in American history or for other societies today. But the life-cycle explanation, as developed by Campbell and his colleagues, does not take politics adequately into account. Partisan loyalties may grow stronger throughout the life cycle, if political conditions reinforce party ties. Apparently, conditions in postwar America did not. Yet, this analysis does not allow us to specify those conditions that contribute to developing strong party loyalties. Although it strongly suggests that conditions in the 1920s and 1930s were far more conducive to developing party loyalties than those during the postwar years, we do not know what it was about those earlier conditions that encouraged partisan ties. I strongly suspect that the differences between these eras are largely political, but television—the long-term effects of which are difficult to measure—also may have contributed to the decline of partisanship. Such questions may be answered best through cross-national research that allows us to discriminate between alternative explanations.

If political conditions did erode party loyalties, future conditions might strengthen partisanship. If such conditions occurred during the next decade, we would expect partisan loyalties to grow stronger, especially among younger cohorts relatively open to partisan change. A generational explanation suggests that the strength of partisan loyalties would then no longer increase directly with age, for partisanship would be strongest among the oldest and youngest cohorts. But this proposition can be tested only if political conditions that strengthen party loyalties do, in fact, occur.

It seems far more likely that future American party loyalties will be weak. The prewar electorate, which still has strong party ties, is being replaced continuously by voters who have weak party loyalties, and we have no evidence that the young will become more partisan as they age. But regardless of future partisan loyalties, these findings are important because they shed light on one process through which party loyalties among mass electorates gradually are transformed: a process of generational change in which the partisan loyalties among older generations tend to persist, although older generations gradually are replaced by new generations that have attitudes different from their elders.

Notes

1. Angus Campbell, et al., *The American Voter*, (New York: Wiley, 1960), p. 121.

2. Ibid., p. 122.

3. These arguments are advanced by Campbell, et al., *The American Voter*, pp. 120-45, and in several essays in the volume by the same authors, *Elections and the Political Order* (New York: Wiley, 1966).

4. For example, see Donald D. Searing, Joel J. Schwartz, and Alden E. Lind, "The Structuring Principle: Political Socialization and Belief Systems," *American Political Science Review*, 67 (June 1973): 415-32; and W. Phillips Shively, "Party Identification, Party Choice, and Voting Stability: The Weimar Case," *American Political Science Review*, 66 (December 1972): 1203-25.

5. For example, see the extensive discussion of this research literature in David O. Sears, "Political Socialization," in *Handbook of Political Science. Volume 2: Theoretical Aspects of Micropolitics*, ed. Fred I. Greenstein and Nelson W. Polsby (Reading, Massachusetts: Addison-Wesley, 1975), in press.

6. Campbell, et al., *The American Voter*, p. 161.

7. Ibid., p. 161.

8. Ibid.

9. Ibid.

10. Ibid., p. 163. For a similar analysis examining the relationship between age and strength of partisanship in Britain, see Butler and Stokes, *Political Change in Britain: Forces Shaping Electoral Choice* (New York: St. Martin's, 1969), pp. 56-57.

11. See Edward C. Dreyer, "Change and Stability in Party Identifications," *Journal of Politics*, 35 (August 1973): 712-22.

12. See David S. Broder, *The Party's Over: The Failure of Politics in America* (New York: Harper and Row, 1972). For another provocative discussion, see Walter Dean Burnham, "The End of American Party Politics," *Trans-action*, 7 (December 1969): 12-22.

13. See Norval D. Glenn and Ted Hefner, "Further Evidence on Aging and

Party Identification," *Public Opinion Quarterly*, 36 (Spring 1972): 31-47; and Norval D. Glenn, "Sources of Shift to Political Independence: Some Evidence from a Cohort Analysis," *Social Science Quarterly*, 53 (December 1972): 494-519.

14. Glenn and Hefner, "Further Evidence on Aging," p. 44.

15. M. Kent Jennings and Richard G. Niemi, "Continuity and Change in Political Orientations: A Longitudinal Study of Two Generations," paper presented at the 69th annual meeting of the American Political Science Association, New Orleans, Louisiana, September, 1973.

16. Ibid., p. 14.

17. Ibid.

18. For example, in France there was a sharp rise in the percentage of party identifiers between 1958 and 1968, even among older cohorts. See Ronald Inglehart and Avram Hochstein, "Alignment and Dealignment of the Electorate in France and the United States," *Comparative Political Studies*, 5 (October 1972): 343-72. Inglehart and Hochstein also used SRC data collected in 1958 and 1968 to conduct a cohort analysis of partisan change in the United States.

19. Philip E. Converse discusses the changing proportion of apoliticals in "Change in the American Electorate," in *The Human Meaning of Social Change*, at p. 306. As Converse notes, most black apoliticals lived in the South.

5 Towards a New Coalition?

The decline of class voting and partisan loyalties may lead to new partisan alignments. Party leaders who do not feel tied to class-based politics may be freer to exploit new issues and to mobilize new sources of support. Voters who feel only weak loyalties to the established parties may more readily discard their allegiances and turn toward parties and candidates that present attractive appeals. But race is the one enduring cleavage that divides the American electorate. The importance of racial conflict may wax and wane, but a highly mobilized black electorate is the most dramatic new fact of postwar politics. A new partisan alignment cannot be based on race alone, for pragmatism prevents any major party from embracing blacks as the major component of their coalition. Yet blacks may have allies who could forge coalitions with them. A cohort analysis of attitudinal differences suggests that relatively privileged whites may be the most likely to form such a coalition. Several writers have suggested that a coalition between white elites and blacks may be emerging.

David Apter develops this thesis at a high level of abstraction.[1] According to Apter, a growing number of persons in advanced industrial societies cannot contribute to economic growth, either because they lack the skills to do so, or because they are excluded from the productive process by prejudice against their race, religion, or ethnic group. Apter labels these people "functionally superfluous," although he recognizes they are superfluous to the economy because of conditions largely beyond their control. The technologically competent, with the skills and abilities to contribute to economic growth, are at the higher end of the stratification hierarchy. They are internally differentiated. On the one hand, there is a theory-generating class that produces new information and an administrative class that consumes information in order to uphold established norms; on the other hand, there are bourgeois radicals who reject society's increasing emphasis upon materialistic goals. These groups, Apter argues, compete to form links with the functionally superfluous.

The technologically obsolescent, who still contribute to economic growth, but whose skills are decreasing in value, occupy the middle ranks in this stratification hierarchy. According to Apter, the technologically obsolescent often develop conservative or reactionary values to compensate for their declining economic importance. The technologically obsolescent do not form a cohesive class, for they are internally differentiated and often have differing short-term goals. Moreover, it is difficult to establish upper and lower boundaries between the obsolescent and the superfluous and between the obsolescent and the competent. I use the term middle stratum, suggesting that this group is not cohesive, to describe them. The middle group, according to Apter, is composed of numerous subgroups held together by many criteria. Persons within the middle stratum, Apter argues, attempt to form short-term coalitions. In an advanced industrial society, coalitions continually change.

Apter's thesis is highly suggestive and can be used to examine changes in the United States.[a] However, the United States is an atypical advanced industrial society, for the functionally superfluous are disproportionately black. But even though blacks make up more than their share of the unskilled, a majority of the functionally superfluous is white. Race is the most important social attribute in the United States, and the functionally superfluous are racially heterogeneous. The least skilled whites seldom support black demands, and the functionally superfluous thus are divided. Moreover, blacks, regardless of their technological competence, are likely to behave politically on the basis of their race.

Although blacks are more difficult to organize than whites, their leaders make demands. Two demands potentially threaten middle stratum whites—that blacks receive preferential treatment in employment and that poor blacks (as well as poor whites) receive substantial welfare payments. Demands for employment opportunities threaten to take away jobs from middle-stratum whites. In addition, many persons in the middle stratum do hard, tedious work for relatively little reward and do not wish others to receive substantial rewards without working for them. But to persons who are highly skilled, and thus relatively secure, black demands may seem reasonable. Their jobs are seldom threatened. Although they do not want to pay higher taxes to provide welfare, they often support policies to improve opportunities for blacks. Persons in the middle stratum resent the technologically competent, especially the bourgeois radicals, for supporting black demands. They also resent the technologically competent for their conspicuous disregard for middle stratum norms, especially those norms that have been codified into law. As universities are often the most conspicuous symbol of the upper stratum, persons in the middle stratum often resent them.

Walter Dean Burnham reformulates Apter's thesis and provides considerable evidence that upper-middle class whites have formed electoral coalitions with blacks. "There is a good deal of evidence," Burnham wrote in 1970, "that the past few years have been marked by a redefinition of American politics in which the alliance between the top and bottom of the new stratification pattern has become increasingly met by countermobilization within the threatened middle."[2] Burnham interprets the 1972 election as a triumph of the threatened middle. There has been, he argues, "Profound modification of the class structure under conditions of technological transformation and affluence. Very generally,

---

[a]The following two paragraphs are my own reformulation of Apter's thesis. Apter specifically discusses political changes in the United States in, "Radicalization and Embourgeoisement: Hypotheses for a Comparative Study of History," *The Journal of Interdisciplinary History*, 1 (Winter 1971), 265-303.

the modifications parallel those suggested some years ago by David Apter, with an emergent stratification of the technologically-competent, technologically-obsolescent, and technologically-superfluous being superimposed upon the older industrial stratification pattern."[3] And Burnham continues, "With the nomination of George McGovern, cleavages within the population have been explicitly organized at the national level around these changes in *society* which have undermined the basis of the old New Deal alignment."[4]

Apter's thesis is too complex to be tested either with the survey data I use or with the aggregate voting data Burnham employs. To operationalize Apter's categories one would need to know precisely what skills each individual possessed as well as what skills were becoming obsolescent in a rapidly changing, complex industrial society. Among the numerous potential indicators of skill available with the recent Michigan surveys, level of education provides the single most valid indicator. Knowledge, Apter argues, is the dynamic element of advanced industrial societies, and formal education imparts theoretical knowledge. Of course, some persons with little formal education will have economically valuable skills, but they will often be skills specific to a single type of job, and which may be rendered obsolescent by technological change. Highly educated persons possess the literacy skills that allow them to be more flexible as the economy changes. A person's level of formal education will not necessarily correlate with his or her ability to contribute to the economy, though, for other factors, such as his or her physical or mental health, and simply luck itself, affect a person's capabilities. Nevertheless, level of education can be used as a simple indicator to differentiate among persons at different levels in the stratification hierarchy.

Given the variety of measures used in the recent Michigan surveys, one can choose among several indicators to measure distinctions within the middle and upper stratum. Level of occupation (using, for example, the Duncan measure of socioeconomic status) or reported annual family income might be a valid measure, but there are problems with both when one is examining differences between age groups. Many young aspiring professionals and upper-level managers begin their careers in the lower ranks. Yet, given his skill at manipulating concepts, a young junior executive may have high, and often realistic, expectations about future success. Income may be a misleading measure, for many young skilled manual workers may earn more than young future professionals, for manual workers attain their peak incomes when they are relatively young. For these reasons, level of education may be a more valid measure of a person's location within the new stratification hierarchy than his family income or occupational attainment. Using level of education also allows us to rank women according to their own attainment, rather than relying upon measures of their husbands' success.

But education, too, presents problems once age comparisons are made. Only a few decades ago, persons without educational credentials had greater opportunities to move into the upper stratum. One could attempt to build additive measures of stratification ranking, but such procedures raise problems of interaction effects resulting from status inconsistency. On balance, none of the available measures is adequate to operationalize Apter's categories fully. I proceed on the assumption that a preliminary test of his thesis should rely upon a simple measure that can be understood easily. And level of education is the single most valid measure of his categories.

This chapter demonstrates that the attitudinal basis for an alignment between upper-stratum whites and blacks may be emerging. I will examine attitudes toward minority groups, urban unrest, and campus unrest, as well as feelings toward social groups. The evidence shows that college-educated whites are more likely to have the same attitudes and dispositions as blacks than are whites with less formal education. Moreover, attitudinal polarization is stronger among young whites than among their elders, suggesting that polarization among whites may be increasing. In the next chapter I will continue my cohort analysis to demonstrate that these attitudes and feelings may contribute to new partisan alignments.

**Attitudes Among Age Cohorts
in 1970 and 1972**

In 1968 the University of Michigan researchers began to use attitudinal measures to locate the respondent in a "space" defined by current social issues. Interviewers posed a basic policy problem, stated two polar solutions, and asked the respondent to rank his own position on a seven-point scale. In 1968 only two spatial questions were asked. One measured policy attitudes toward Vietnam, the other attitudes toward urban unrest. By 1970 eight spatial questions were employed, three of which are central to our discussion. Persons were asked whether the government in Washington should aid minority groups or whether minority groups should help themselves, whether the best way to deal with urban unrest was to solve the problems of poverty or to use all available force, and whether they felt sympathetic with student and faculty demonstrators or whether the police and national guard should be used to stop campus disturbances. The full questions, all of which were repeated in 1972, were as follows:

"Some people feel that the government in Washington should make every possible effort to improve the social and economic position of Negroes [in 1972, Blacks] and other minority groups. Others feel that the government should not make any special effort to help minorities because they should help themselves. . . . Where would you place yourself on this scale, or haven't you thought much about this?"

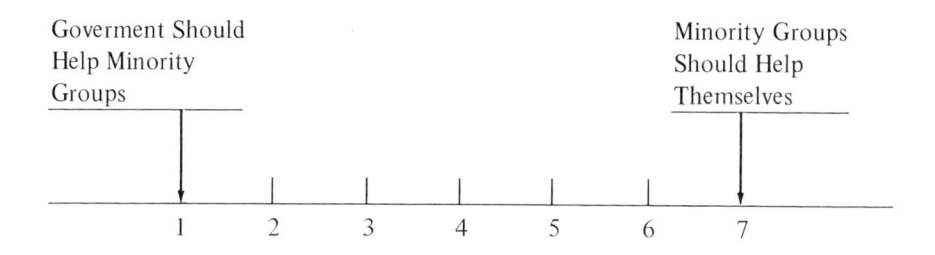

Goverment Should							Minority Groups
Help Minority							Should Help
Groups							Themselves
↓						↓	
—	—	—	—	—	—	—
1	2	3	4	5	6	7

"There is much discussion about the best way to deal with the problem of urban unrest and rioting. Some say it is more important to use all available force to maintain law and order—no matter what the results Others say it is more important to correct the problems of poverty and unemployment that give rise to the disturbances. . . . Where would you place yourself on this scale, or haven't you thought much about this?"

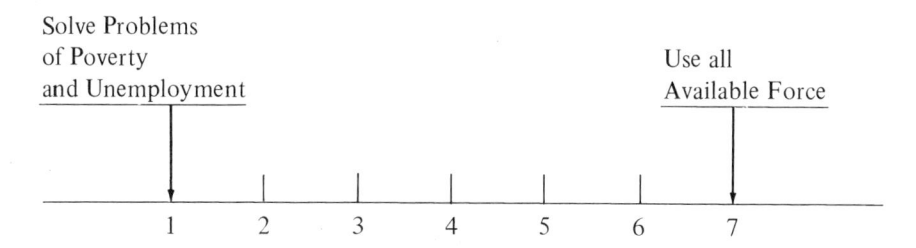

Solve Problems						Use all
of Poverty						Available Force
and Unemployment						
↓						↓
—	—	—	—	—	—	—
1	2	3	4	5	6	7

"Some people are pretty upset about rioting and disturbances on college campuses and in high schools. Some feel sympathetic with the students and faculty who take part in these disturbances; others think the schools should use police and the national guard to prevent or stop disturbances, and others fall somewhere between these extremes. . . . Where would you place yourself on this scale, or haven't you thought much about this?"

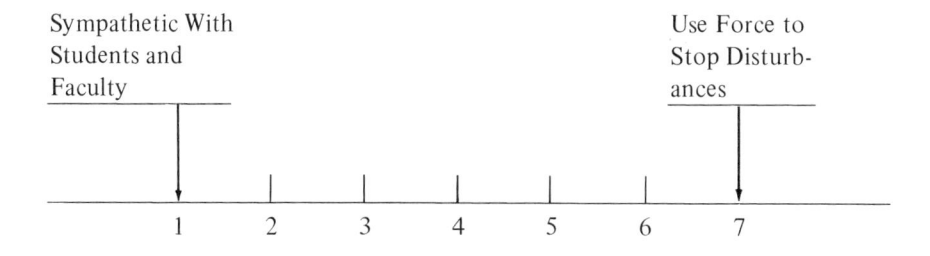

Sympathetic With						Use Force to
Students and						Stop Disturb-
Faculty						ances
↓						↓
—	—	—	—	—	—	—
1	2	3	4	5	6	7

These three items seem to tap attitudes central to our discussion. The question about aiding minority groups is useful for it does not tap a simple racial dimension, but also measures the respondent's attitude toward government involvement in the economy. Persons who favor solving the problems of poverty to deal with urban unrest are more sympathetic with the functionally superfluous than those who advocate using all available force to maintain law and order. And persons who favor using the police and national guard to quell campus unrest are more hostile toward bourgeois radicals than those who sympathize with student and faculty demonstrators.

In both 1970 and 1972 the responses to these questions were strongly interrelated. Persons who tended toward aiding minority groups were more likely to favor solving the problems of poverty as a solution for urban unrest and were more likely to sympathize with students and faculty. Acceptable Guttman scales can be built with these items, but as my analysis is highly exploratory, I present a separate analysis for each item.

Although these three items are central to our thesis, there were other items that might have been used. In 1970, in addition to the three items I analyzed, the SRC asked spatial questions about Vietnam, government policy toward inflation, the importance of protecting the rights of the accused, government policy toward pollution, and government health insurance. As Jerrold G. Rusk and Herbert F. Weisberg have reported, responses to questions about Vietnam and toward the rights of the accused correlated highly with attitudes toward government aid for minority groups, urban unrest, and campus unrest.[5] But these two items did not seem central to the hypotheses I was testing. The question about protecting the rights of the accused might tap attitudes toward the functionally superfluous, who are more often charged with crimes. But the question more directly taps attitudes toward civil liberties. In 1972 the SRC again increased the number of spatial policy questions, including potentially useful questions about the legalization of marijuana, busing, and equality for women. But my basic research decision was to restrict my analysis to items that were asked in both 1970 and 1972 so that I could determine whether relationships obtained for at least two separate surveys.

There were strong racial differences in the responses to these three basic policy questions. Blacks were much more likely to favor government aid for minority groups than whites were; they were more likely to favor solving the problems of poverty as a solution for urban unrest; and, perhaps surprisingly, they were more sympathetic toward students and faculty. In 1970 only 25 percent of the whites tended toward aiding minority groups; 27 percent were neutral; and 48 percent felt minority groups should help themselves;[b] among blacks, 84 percent tended toward aiding minority groups. In 1972, 29 percent of

---

[b]Throughout this discussion, persons scoring 1, 2, and 3 are considered to tend toward the liberal position, those scoring 4 as tending to be neutral, and those scoring 5, 6, and 7 as tending toward the conservative position.

the whites tended toward government aid for minority groups; 25 percent took a neutral position; and 46 percent felt minority groups should help themselves; among blacks, 78 percent favored government aid. In 1970 whites were about as likely to favor solving the problems of poverty as using force to solve the problem of urban unrest: 38 percent tended toward solving the problems of poverty; 28 percent took a neutral position; and 34 percent tended to favor using all available force; among blacks, 78 percent favored solving the problems of poverty. In 1972 there was a marked shift in favor of solving the problems of poverty: among whites, 57 percent favored solving the problems of poverty; 17 percent took a neutral position; and 25 percent tended toward using all available force; among blacks, 82 percent favored solving the problems of poverty.

Few whites sympathized with student and faculty demonstrators and a clear majority favored using the police and national guard to prevent disturbances. In 1970 only 13 percent of the whites tended to sympathize with student and faculty dissidents; 17 percent were neutral; and 70 percent favored using force to quell campus unrest; among blacks, 56 percent sympathized with students and faculty. In 1972, 18 percent of the whites sympathized with the students and faculty; 25 percent were neutral; and 57 percent favored using force; among blacks, 54 percent were sympathetic with students and faculty.

If our thesis is correct, whites high in the stratification hierarchy will be more likely to support minority group demands than those in the middle and lower end; also, the advantaged will be more likely to sympathize with students and faculty. The data support the thesis. In 1970, among whites who had graduated from college, 38 percent favored aid for minority groups; 52 percent tended toward solving the problems of poverty; and 26 percent were sympathetic with students and faculty. In 1972, 41 percent of the white college graduates favored aiding minority groups, and 31 percent were sympathetic with students and faculty. White college graduates were not more likely to favor solving the problems of poverty (55 percent did), but they were less likely (20 percent) to favor force to solve the problems of urban unrest than were less educated whites. On all three items in 1970, and with two out of the three items in 1972, white college graduates were more likely to approximate the attitudes of blacks than were less educated whites.

It should be recognized that white college graduates were much more likely to share the views of less educated whites than they were to share the views of blacks. But further specification of these findings shows that, among the college educated, the young were much more likely to approximate the attitudes of blacks than were their elders. In examining the relationship of attitudes by level of education among age groups, I divided the electorate into three basic cohorts. The prewar cohort was born before 1924. The postwar cohort was divided into two subgroups—the 1924 to 1939 age group and the post-Eisenhower cohort born in 1940 and after. The post-Eisenhower cohort was the age group among whom there was a negative relationship between social class and direction of presidential vote in both 1968 and 1972 and among whom there was virtually no relationship between social class and direction of party identification in 1968, 1970, and 1972. Tables 5-1 and 5-2 present the distribution of respondents by level of education and years of birth.[c] Tables 5-3 and 5-4 show the attitudes of each cohort of whites and of blacks, and the attitudes of whites among each educational level within each age cohort.[d]

In both 1970 and 1972 there were modest age differences in attitudes among whites. The young were more likely to favor aid to minority groups, solving the problems of poverty, and were more likely to sympathize with student and faculty demonstrators. The liberal attitudes of the young partly result from their higher level of education. Highly educated whites are more liberal, and among the younger cohorts, the proportion of highly educated whites is much greater than among the prewar cohort. But the liberalism of the young is not just the result of their higher levels of education; it also occurs because the highly educated young are much more liberal than their comparably educated elders. In fact, among whites lacking any college education, there are no consistent age-group differences. These findings lead us to modify any simple thesis that there are fundamental conflicts over values *between* generations. Such conflicts may exist, but only among relatively well-educated whites. While any simple generation gap thesis must be modified,[6] the liberalism of the highly educated young may have special social impact, for they are highly articulate and may have political influence out of proportion to their numbers.

In both 1970 and 1972 white college graduates born in 1940 and after were more likely than any other group of whites to favor aiding minority groups and the most likely to sympathize with student and faculty demonstrators. And in

---

[c]These distributions are provided so that the reader may approximate the numbers upon which the percentages and mean scores in the subsequent tables are based. As all the questions I used for the 1972 survey were asked in the post-election interview, I report distributions for the post-election survey.

The numbers upon which percentages are based are always somewhat lower than those reported in Tables 5-1 and 5-2, for they are based only upon persons who gave a meaningful response. In addition, in 1972 the questions about solving the problems of poverty and about student and faculty disturbances were asked of only one-half the sample. The post-election question about aiding minority groups was included in a mail questionnaire used to gain data from respondents who could not be reinterviewed. (A total of 94 of these questionnaires was included.) The two other policy items, as well as the "thermometer" questions, were not included in the mail questionnaire.

[d]Some persons among the cohort born in 1940 and after were too young to be college graduates, and some persons included in these tables as having some college are likely to become graduates. Such a misclassification probably tends to reduce the relationship between level of education and attitudes among the young and thus should introduce biases that make it more difficult to support the hypotheses we are testing.

Another bias was introduced by reporting the percentages based only upon those persons who gave a meaningful response. "Don't know" and "haven't thought about it" responses were more frequent among persons with low levels of education. As we report the percentage who tend in the liberal direction, we artificially raise the liberalism of the lower educated whites. This bias, too, makes it more difficult to support the hypotheses we are testing.

Table 5-1
Distribution of Respondents in 1970, by Level of Education, Years of Birth, and Race

Race:			White			
Level of Education:	Eight Grades or Less	Some High School	High School Graduate	Some College	College Graduate	All Educational Levels[a]
Years of Birth:						
Before 1924	251	104	192	63	58	670
1924-1939	49	55	142	62	54	363
1940-1952	6	49	157	92	56	360
Race:			Black			
Years of Birth:						
Before 1924	39	11	12	1	2	66
1924-1939	9	18	9	1	1	38
1940-1952	2	16	26	5	1	50

[a] Including respondents for whom level of education is not reported.

Table 5-2
Distribution of Respondents in 1972, by Level of Education, Years of Birth, and Race[a]

Race: Level of Education:	Eight Grades or Less	Some High School	High School Graduate	Some College	College Graduate	All Educational Levels[b]
			White			
Years of Birth:						
Before 1924	287	185	211	77	72	833
1924-1939	54	77	211	97	106	545
1940-1954	30	85	247	171	112	646
Race:			Black			
Years of Birth:						
Before 1924	39	21	5	4	2	71
1924-1939	13	21	22	9	5	70
1940-1954	8	16	30	12	11	77

[a]Respondents in post-election survey.
[b]Including respondents for whom level of education is not reported.

Table 5-3
Political Attitudes in 1970, by Level of Education, Years of Birth, and Race[a]

Race:	White						White	Black
Level of Education:	Eight Grades or Less	Some High School	High School Graduate	Some College	College Graduate	Relationship Between Attitude and Level of Education Among Whites[b]	All Educational Levels	All Educational Levels
Percentage who tend toward aiding minority groups, by years of birth:								
Before 1924	21%	13%	18%	25%	29%	.08	20%	83%
1924-1939	18%	13%	22%	39%	40%	.20	26%	86%
1940-1952	(1) (6)	11%	28%	37%	45%	.17	31%	81%
Percentage who tend toward solving problems of poverty, by years of birth:								
Before 1924	32%	34%	37%	33%	44%	.04	35%	82%
1924-1939	26%	16%	39%	42%	59%	.15	37%	76%
1940-1952	(1) (6)	47%	38%	48%	55%	.10	44%	76%
Percentage who tend toward sympathy with student and faculty demonstrators, by years of birth:								
Before 1924	7%	4%	9%	16%	18%	.14	9%	54%
1924-1939	7%	8%	9%	18%	23%	.19	12%	56%
1940-1952	(1) (6)	16%	9%	33%	36%	.17	20%	59%

[a]To approximate the Ns upon which these percentages are based, see Table 5-1.
[b]Kendall's tau-c relationship between a five-fold ordinal measure of education as listed above and a seven-fold ordinal measure of attitude described on pp. 74-75.

Table 5-4
Political Attitudes in 1972, by Level of Education, Years of Birth, and Race[a]

Race:	White						White	Black
Level of Education:	Eight Grades or Less	Some High School	High School Graduate	Some College	College Graduate	Relationship Between Attitude and Level of Education Among Whites[b]	All Educational Levels	All Educational Levels
Percentage who tend toward aiding minority groups, by years of birth:								
Before 1924	23%	23%	22%	32%	26%	.12	24%	76%
1924-1939	18%	18%	20%	30%	42%	.19	26%	76%
1940-1954	26%	31%	32%	40%	50%	.17	37%	82%
Percentage who tend toward solving problems of poverty, by years of birth:[c]								
Before 1924	52%	49%	42%	52%	30%	−.03	47%	67%
1924-1939	56%	60%	59%	63%	56%	−.01	59%	87%
1940-1954	(3) (6)	56%	72%	69%	68%	.01	68%	87%
Percentage who tend toward sympathy with student and faculty demonstrators, by years of birth:[c]								
Before 1924	11%	13%	14%	15%	10%	.10	13%	39%
1924-1939	13%	15%	9%	13%	27%	.16	14%	52%
1940-1954	(1) (8)	11%	20%	34%	45%	.18	28%	63%

[a]To approximate the Ns upon which these percentages are based, see Table 5-2.
[b]Kendall's tau-c relationship between a five-fold ordinal measure of education as listed above and a seven-fold ordinal measure of attitude described on pp. 74-75.
[c]These items were asked of only half the sample.

both years these young college graduates were among the most likely to favor solving the problems of poverty as a solution for urban unrest. In both 1970 and 1972 white college graduates born between 1924 and 1939 were more likely to favor aiding minority groups and to sympathize with students and faculty than their less educated age-group peers. In 1970 they were more likely to favor solving the problems of poverty than any other group of whites. White college graduates born before 1924, however, were not consistently more liberal than their less educated age-group peers.

In 1970 there were only negligible age differences among blacks, but in 1972 blacks born after 1923 were much more likely than prewar blacks to tend toward solving the problems of poverty and to sympathize with students and faculty. In 1970 white college graduates born in 1940 and after were more likely to approximate the attitudes of their black age-group peers to minority group aid and toward campus unrest than was any other group of whites; they were among the most likely to approximate the attitudes of their black age-group peers toward urban unrest. In spite of the Leftward shift among young blacks in 1972, a similar pattern persisted. On two of the three policy questions, young white college graduates were more likely to approximate the attitudes of their black age-group peers than other whites were. In both 1970 and 1972 young white college graduates were more likely to approximate the overall attitudes of blacks to minority group aid and to student and faculty demonstrators than were any other groups of whites; in both years they were among the most likely to approximate the overall attitudes of blacks toward urban unrest. Thus, there was at least an attitudinal basis for a coalition of young college-educated whites and of blacks, an alliance that many suggest formed the basis for McGovern's unsuccessful candidacy.

These data also suggest that attitudinal polarization among whites may be increasing. Tables 5-3 and 5-4 present the Kendall's tau-c relationship between a five-fold ordinal measure of education and a seven-fold measure of policy attitudes. The higher the relationship, the greater the tendency for the more highly educated whites to be more liberal than the less educated. In 1970 the relationship between attitudes and level of education was consistently greater among both groups of postwar whites than among prewar whites. Level of education was unrelated to attitudes toward urban unrest in 1972, but the relationships between level of education and attitudes toward minority group aid and campus unrest were stronger among the two postwar cohorts than among the prewar cohort. These data support the findings of other survey researchers who discovered that on race-related issues, polarization by educational level was greater among young whites than among their elders.[7] We cannot determine whether these differences result from generational change or from life-cycle effects until data covering more years become available. But the Leftward leanings of the young college educated may result, at least in part, from the freedom from economic concerns that has characterized the socialization of these privileged young Americans.[8]

Feelings Toward Social Groups Among
Age Cohorts in 1970 and 1972

Since 1964 the SRC has used a thermometer technique to measure "feelings" toward social groups. If a respondent felt very "warm" toward a group, he could give it a score of 100°, if he felt very "cold," a score of 0°. There were intermediate positions between these poles, and a neutral position received a score of 50°. The feeling thermometer questions were posed as follows:

"We'd like to get your feelings toward the candidates for national office in this year's election, using the feeling thermometer we showed you in our earlier interview [the preelection interview]. As you may recall, if you don't feel particularly warm *or* cold toward a candidate, then you should place him in the middle of the thermometer, at 50 degrees. If you have a warm feeling toward a candidate, or feel favorably toward him, you would give him a score somewhere between 50 and 100 degrees. If you don't feel favorably toward a candidate, then you would place him somewhere between 0 and 50 degrees...

"We'd also like to get your feelings about some groups in American society, using the feeling thermometer just as we did for the candidates. If we come to a group you don't know much about, just tell me and we'll move on to the next one...."

The basic thermometer presented to each respondent is displayed in Figure 5-1.

In 1970 the number of groups measured was greatly increased. Eleven are particularly relevant to our thesis that an attitudinal alignment between upper-stratum whites and blacks may be emerging—black militants, urban rioters, radical students, whites, the military, policemen, civil rights leaders, ministers who lead protest marches, Negroes,[e] the women's liberation movement, and people who use marijuana. Feelings toward black militants, urban rioters, civil rights leaders, ministers who lead protest marches, and Negroes may measure attitudes toward minority groups, whereas radical students, women's liberationists, and marijuana smokers represent the counterculture. Whites, the military, and the police may represent established authority.

As this measurement technique is novel, I further explored the meaning of these items by conducting a factor analysis to determine how many attitudinal dimensions they measured.[f] A factor analysis of the white electorate in 1970 and 1972 demonstrated that in both years feelings toward whites, the military, and policemen formed a distinct attitudinal dimension, which may be labelled support for established authorities. Feelings toward radical students, black militants, and urban rioters also formed a clear attitudinal dimension in both

---
[e]In 1972 the word Blacks was used rather than Negroes.

[f]I employed the SPSS program for principal factoring with iteration, using a varimax rotation. See Norman H. Nie, Dale H. Bent, and C. Hadlai Hull, *SPSS: Statistical Package for the Social Sciences* (New York: McGraw Hill, 1970), pp. 208-25.

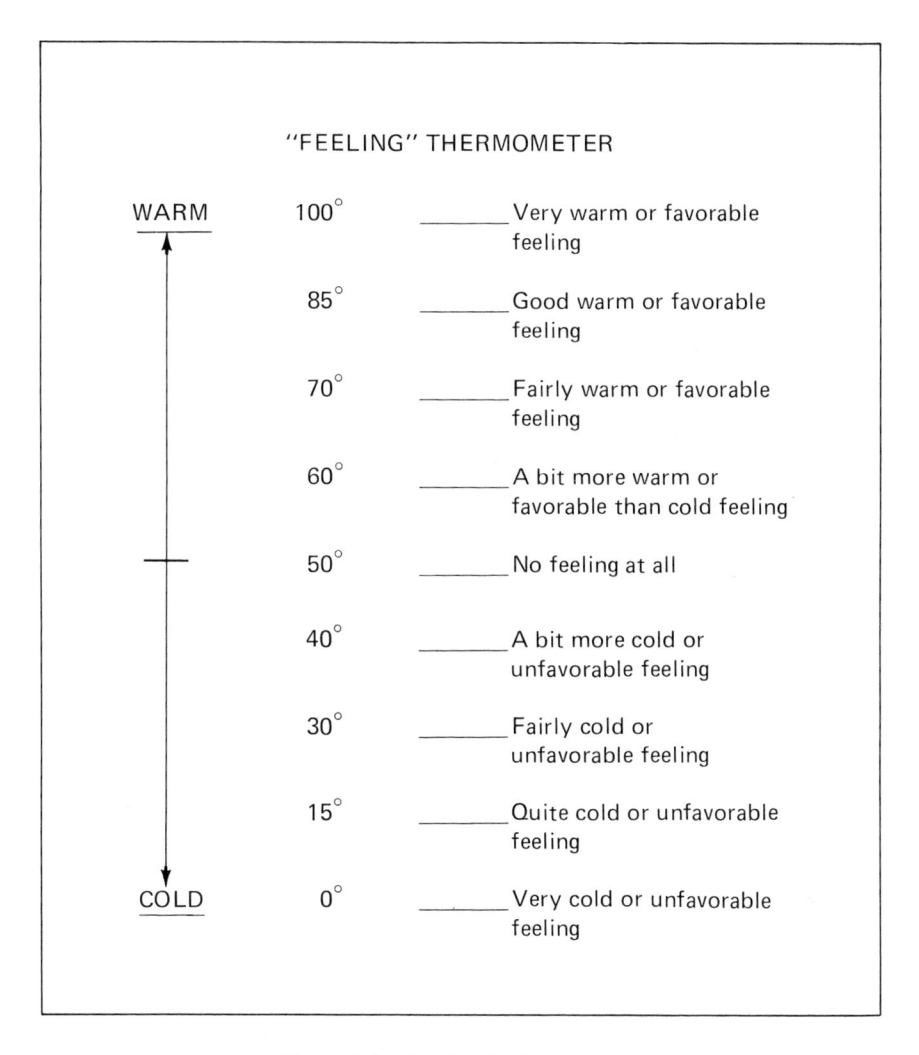

```
                    "FEELING" THERMOMETER

        WARM        100°        _____ Very warm or favorable
                                        feeling

                     85°        _____ Good warm or favorable
                                        feeling

                     70°        _____ Fairly warm or favorable
                                        feeling

                     60°        _____ A bit more warm or
                                        favorable than cold feeling

                     50°        _____ No feeling at all

                     40°        _____ A bit more cold or
                                        unfavorable feeling

                     30°        _____ Fairly cold or
                                        unfavorable feeling

                     15°        _____ Quite cold or unfavorable
                                        feeling

        COLD          0°        _____ Very cold or unfavorable
                                        feeling
```

Figure 5-1. "Feeling" Thermometer

surveys, and appear to measure feelings toward protest. Feelings toward civil rights leaders and Negroes formed a separate factor in 1970, but not in 1972. Several items seemed to measure more than one attitude. For example, feelings toward ministers who lead protests related closely to feelings toward civil rights leaders, but they also related to feelings about protest. Likewise, persons who felt warmly toward marijuana users tended to approve of protestors, but they also felt warmly toward black militants. Given the interrelationships among these items, one could construct indices measuring support for established authorities and sympathy with protest.[g] But, because my study is exploratory, and because these items are intrinsically interesting, I present an item analysis.[h]

If our thesis is correct, technologically competent whites should be more supportive of minorities than are the technologically obsolescent, and they should be more sympathetic toward the counterculture. The technologically obsolescent should more strongly embrace conservative norms, and thus more strongly support established authorities. And, as with our analysis of policy items, we would expect strong racial differences.

Strong racial differences did emerge. The mean scores of whites and blacks toward these eleven groups are presented in Tables 5-5 and 5-6.[i] Racial differences were most pronounced on items directly bearing upon race. In both 1970 and 1972 blacks were much warmer than whites toward civil rights leaders, ministers who lead protest marches, black militants, and Negroes. But blacks were also warmer than whites toward most groups representing the counterculture. Although differences between the races were not great, blacks were somewhat cooler than whites toward groups representing established authorities, although they were almost as warm toward the military as whites were. On only one item, feelings toward marijuana users, were blacks almost identical to whites.

We are not concerned with racial differences per se, but the extent to which the technologically competent whites approximate the feelings of blacks. In both 1970 and 1972 white college graduates came closer than any other group of whites to approximating the attitudes of blacks on nine of the 11 items. The two exceptions were feelings toward the military and toward marijuana users: in both years white college graduates were cooler than blacks toward the military

---

[g]These items have been used to form indices in the past. For example, Teresa E. Levitin and Warren E. Miller, after conducting a cluster analysis, combined the responses to the questions about the military, policemen, and whites to measure support for "agents of social control." Feelings toward radical students, marijuana users, and rock festival attenders were combined to measure attitudes toward the counterculture. (The question about rock festival attenders was not repeated in 1972.) (See "The New Politics and Partisan Realignment," paper presented at the 68th annual meeting of the American Political Science Association, Washington, D.C., September, 1972, pp. 4-6.) Arthur H. Miller, Warren E. Miller, Alden S. Raine, and Thad A. Brown combined thermometer ratings toward radical students, the women's liberation movement, marijuana users, ministers who lead protests, big business, the military, policemen, and whites to form a cultural orientation index. (See "A Majority Party in Disarray: Policy Polarization in the 1972 Election," paper presented at the 69th annual meeting of the American Political Science Association, New Orleans, September, 1973, pp. 59-61.)

[h]In 1972 the SRC added some additional items that might have been useful for testing my thesis, for example, feelings toward poor people and feelings toward intellectuals. I did not use these items, however, for, as with my analysis of the spatial questions, I restricted my inquiry to items that were included in both the 1970 and 1972 surveys.

[i]Persons scoring 98, 99, or 100 degrees were coded as 97. Thus, the means I report are marginally lower than the actual means.

Table 5-5
Feelings Toward Groups in 1970, by Race

Race:	White	Black	Difference Between Races
$\bar{X}$ Feeling Toward:			
Whites	77.7	64.8	−12.9
The Military	72.8	68.3	−4.5
Policemen	79.9	70.4	−9.5
Black Militants	10.0	38.9	+28.9
People Who Riot in Cities	6.8	26.5	+19.7
Radical Students	12.1	29.7	+17.6
Civil Rights Leaders	41.8	80.0	+38.2
Ministers Who Lead Protest Marches	24.7	63.8	+39.1
Negroes	58.7	86.4	+27.7
Women's Liberation Movement	31.4	46.3	+14.9
People Who Use Marijuana	12.0	14.7	+2.7

Table 5-6
Feelings Toward Groups in 1972, by Race

Race:	White	Black	Difference Between Races
$\bar{X}$ Feeling Toward:			
Whites	78.9	64.7	−14.2
The Military	69.9	67.0	−2.9
Policemen	76.5	65.7	−10.8
Black Militants	15.0	41.8	+26.8
People Who Riot in Cities	10.6	28.1	+17.5
Radical Students	24.6	42.9	+18.3
Civil Rights Leaders	36.8	78.5	+41.7
Ministers Who Lead Protest Marches	32.5	68.7	+36.2
Blacks	61.0	88.3	+27.3
Women's Liberation Movement	44.3	56.9	+12.6
People Who Use Marijuana	21.0	21.7	+0.7

and warmer than blacks toward people who used marijuana. It should be recognized that on some items white college graduates were much more likely to share the feelings of less educated whites than they were to share those of blacks. For example, in both years white college graduates more closely resembled poorly educated whites than blacks in their feelings toward black militants and toward Negroes. On the other hand, college-educated whites were more likely to have the same feelings as blacks toward whites and toward policemen. On most of these items, however, white college graduates had feelings about halfway between those of poorly educated whites and those of blacks.

Tables 5-7 and 5-8 present the mean feelings of each cohort of whites and of blacks, and the mean score of whites among each educational level within each cohort.[j] They also show the Kendall's tau-b relationship between a five-fold measure of education and a five-fold ordinal measure of feeling.[k] A high relationship indicates that level of education is strongly related to the direction of feelings within the age cohort.[l] These data reveal consistent age differences among whites. In both years the young were more likely to feel warmly toward black protestors and toward the counterculture, more likely to feel cooly toward symbols of established authority. Only the responses to one item, feelings toward Negroes (blacks, in 1972), were unrelated to age. The liberal feelings of the young resulted partly from their higher levels of education. Once again, the more highly-educated whites were more liberal than the less well educated, and overall levels of education were higher among the younger cohorts. But the liberalism of the young was not just the result of their higher levels of education. It also occurs because the highly educated young differed markedly from their comparably educated elders. In fact, in 1970 there were no consistent differences between age groups among whites lacking some college education, and in 1972 there were no consistent age differences among whites who were not at least high school graduates. And, it is among white college graduates that age-group differences are sharpest. Once again, we must reject any simple thesis that conflicts *between* generations are emerging. These conflicts exist, but only among relatively highly-educated whites.

Young college graduates differed considerably from most other whites. In both 1970 and 1972 white college graduates born in 1940 and after were the

---

[j]Persons with low levels of education were more likely to give polar responses of 0 or 100 degrees than those with higher levels of education. Unfortunately, I cannot determine whether this results from their lack of sophistication or from their genuine hostility (or enthusiasm) for social groups. To compensate for the possibility of a systematic bias in a direction supporting my hypotheses, I also examined the relationship between level of education and feelings toward groups among cohorts using the arbitrary ordinal categories described below. By grouping all persons below 30 degrees into one category and all those 70 degrees and higher into another, we can compensate somewhat for the tendency of persons with low levels of education to give extreme responses. A contingency table analysis yielded results similar to those obtained using mean scores.

[k]Responses were divided into five ordinal categories: less than 30 degrees; between 30 degrees and 49 degrees; 50 degrees; between 51 degrees and 69 degrees; and 70 degrees and higher. A Kendall's tau-b was used to report the relationships as the correlation matrices had an identical number of columns and rows. (The Kendall's tau-c was used for tables with an unequal number of columns and rows.)

[l]The direction of the relationship for the first three items has been reflected so that the reported correlation is positive if persons with higher levels of education were cooler toward whites, the military, and policemen than were those with lower levels of education.

Table 5-7
Feelings Toward Groups in 1970, by Level of Education, Years of Birth, and Race[a]

Race:			White					White	Black
Level of Education:	Eight Grades or Less	Some High School	High School Graduate	Some College	College Graduate	Relationship Between Feelings and Level of Education Among Whites[b]		All Educational Levels	All Educational Levels
$\bar{X}$ feelings toward whites, by years of birth:									
Before 1924	83	82	76	76	75	.16		80	66
1924-1939	76	74	79	79	66	.04		76	67
1940-1952	†	79	78	75	69	.09		76	62
$\bar{X}$ feelings toward the military, by years of birth:									
Before 1924	79	78	73	70	63	.16		75	71
1924-1939	80	77	77	67	60	.22		73	75
1940-1952	†	78	76	61	49	.30		68	61
$\bar{X}$ feelings toward policemen, by years of birth:									
Before 1924	82	84	81	80	81	−.03		82	72
1924-1939	83	81	81	81	71	.07		80	77
1940-1952	†	80	80	73	70	.11		77	63
$\bar{X}$ feelings toward black militants, by years of birth:									
Before 1924	8	7	5	7	9	−.04		7	29
1924-1939	7	6	8	10	20	.14		10	36
1940-1952	†	15	13	18	22	.13		16	54

Table 5-7 (cont.)

Race: Level of Education:	White					Relationship Between Feelings and Level of Education Among Whites[b]	White All Educational Levels	Black All Educational Levels
	Eight Grades or Less	Some High School	High School Graduate	Some College	College Graduate			

$\bar{X}$ feelings toward people who riot in cities, by years of birth:

Before 1924	4	5	4	5	8	.04	5	21
1924-1939	4	5	5	7	10	.14	6	22
1940-1952	†	8	8	16	19	.21	12	38

$\bar{X}$ feelings toward radical students, by years of birth:

Before 1924	7	8	7	12	16	.10	9	21
1924-1939	4	6	11	14	21	.21	11	28
1940-1952	†	16	15	24	27	.16	19	43

$\bar{X}$ feelings toward civil rights leaders, by years of birth:

Before 1924	34	34	40	45	46	.13	38	80
1924-1939	33	34	42	50	57	.23	43	83
1940-1952	†	38	44	51	57	.20	47	78

$\bar{X}$ feelings toward ministers who lead protest marches, by years of birth:

Before 1924	16	18	21	26	27	.13	20	64
1924-1939	16	14	24	32	41	.26	25	63
1940-1952	†	24	25	43	47	.29	33	64
$\bar{X}$ feelings toward Negroes, by years of birth:								
Before 1924	54	56	58	64	65	.10	58	83
1924-1939	52	53	59	65	66	.17	59	91
1940-1952	†	57	60	63	63	.08	60	86
$\bar{X}$ feelings toward women's liberation movement, by years of birth:								
Before 1924	30	33	29	26	32	.00	30	41
1924-1939	25	29	32	34	36	.09	32	45
1940-1952	†	35	29	37	39	.07	34	54
$\bar{X}$ feelings toward people who use marijuana, by years of birth:								
Before 1924	4	6	7	14	16	.17	7	8
1924-1939	3	5	9	17	27	.32	12	5
1940-1952	†	9	13	34	34	.35	21	31

[a] To approximate the Ns that constitute each subset, see Table 5-1.

[b] Kendall's tau-b relationship between a five-fold ordinal measure of education as listed above and a five-fold ordinal measure of feelings described in note k.

† Because of the small N, mean scores for this subset have not been presented.

Table 5-8
Feelings Toward Groups in 1972, by Level of Education, Years of Birth, and Race[a]

Race:		White					White	Black
Level of Education:	Eight Grades or Less	Some High School	High School Graduate	Some College	College Graduate	Relationship Between Feelings and Level of Education Among Whites[b]	All Educational Levels	All Educational Levels
$\bar{X}$ feelings toward whites, by years of birth:								
Before 1924	86	84	83	81	78	.13	83	68
1924-1939	80	83	80	75	71	.11	78	66
1940-1954	79	81	75	73	69	.11	74	61
$\bar{X}$ feelings toward the military, by years of birth:								
Before 1924	79	79	77	71	70	.08	77	71
1924-1939	79	76	73	70	60	.21	71	68
1940-1954	72	72	64	57	48	.23	61	62
$\bar{X}$ feelings toward policemen, by years of birth:								
Before 1924	81	81	81	81	76	.03	81	69
1924-1939	81	80	77	76	70	.11	76	70
1940-1954	73	78	73	70	64	.15	71	60
$\bar{X}$ feelings toward black militants, by years of birth:								
Before 1924	11	10	10	9	13	-.02	10	24
1924-1939	8	15	12	15	19	.08	14	42
1940-1954	17	20	20	21	26	.08	21	56

$\bar{X}$ feelings toward people who riot in cities, by years of birth:								
Before 1924	7	6	6	6	9	−.03	7	14
1924-1939	4	9	9	9	15	.12	10	28
1940-1954	11	10	15	18	23	.16	16	40
$\bar{X}$ feelings toward radical students, by years of birth:								
Before 1924	20	21	19	18	19	−.03	20	35
1924-1939	18	25	23	23	28	.06	24	40
1940-1954	30	25	30	31	35	.07	31	53
$\bar{X}$ feelings toward civil rights leaders, by years of birth:								
Before 1924	28	23	30	36	39	.10	29	77
1924-1939	19	34	36	44	50	.23	39	77
1940-1954	29	32	40	50	58	.27	44	80
$\bar{X}$ feelings toward ministers who lead protest marches, by years of birth:								
Before 1924	23	21	26	28	34	.10	25	58
1924-1939	18	32	32	37	46	.20	34	73
1940-1954	28	27	38	44	54	.25	41	74
$\bar{X}$ feelings toward blacks, by years of birth:								
Before 1924	59	62	64	62	64	.05	62	89
1924-1939	56	65	63	64	62	.02	63	87
1940-1954	54	58	58	60	61	.06	59	89

Table 5-8 (cont.)

Race: Level of Education:	White Eight Grades or Less	Some High School	High School Graduate	Some College	College Graduate	Relationship Between Feelings and Level of Education Among Whites[b]	White All Educational Levels	Black All Educational Levels
$\bar{X}$ feelings toward women's liberation movement, by years of birth:								
Before 1924	45	43	41	49	40	−.03	44	47
1924-1939	44	43	42	37	47	−.01	42	61
1940-1954	30	45	45	47	57	.15	47	62
$\bar{X}$ feelings toward people who use marijuana, by years of birth:								
Before 1924	11	8	15	17	19	.08	13	10
1924-1939	7	14	16	21	29	.23	18	18
1940-1954	18	18	30	39	47	.26	33	35

[a]To approximate the *N*s that constitute each subset, see Table 5-2.
[b]Kendall's tau-b relationship between a five-fold ordinal measure of education as listed above and a five-fold ordinal measure of feelings described in note k.

subgroup of whites coolest toward the military and toward policemen; in 1970 they were the second coolest subgroup toward whites, and in 1972 they were cooler toward whites than any other subgroup. In both surveys they were the warmest subgroup (or tied for warmest) toward every other group except Negroes. White college graduates born between 1924 and 1939 were consistently cooler toward whites, policemen, and the military than their less educated age-group peers, and they were consistently warmer toward every other group except Negroes. White college graduates born before 1924 were usually cooler toward established authorities and warmer toward other groups than were less educated prewar whites, but these differences were negligible.

Both surveys revealed age-group differences among blacks. In both years blacks born in 1940 and after were cooler toward established authorities than older blacks and were somewhat warmer toward the women's liberation movement; in both surveys blacks born in 1940 and after were much warmer than older blacks toward urban rioters, radical students, and marijuana users. Both surveys showed that blacks born between 1924 and 1939 were markedly warmer toward black militants and toward radical students than were blacks born before 1924. Age-group differences among blacks were often greater than age differences among white college graduates. Because young blacks were often more radical in their feelings than were their elders, young white college graduates were not consistently more likely to approximate the feelings of their black age-group peers. Yet, young white college graduates often came closest to approximating the overall feelings of the black population, and on some items had feelings very similar to those of blacks. For example, in both surveys white college graduates born in 1940 and after had feelings toward policemen virtually identical to those of blacks; they were only marginally warmer toward whites than the overall black population. In 1972 their feelings toward women's liberation were identical to those of blacks. In both surveys their feelings toward urban rioters, radical students, and ministers who lead protest marches were not as warm as blacks', but they came closer to approximating the feelings of blacks than to sharing the overall feelings of the white population. There were other items on which highly-educated whites were more like whites than they were like blacks. And having similar feelings will not necessarily lead highly-educated whites and blacks to share common policy objectives. But these data suggest that there may be the attitudinal basis for a coalition of young college-educated whites and of blacks.

These data, as with those on policy preferences, suggest that polarization among whites may be increasing. In both 1970 and 1972 the relationship between level of education and feelings was greater among both cohorts of postwar whites than among their elders on feelings toward the military, people who riot in cities, civil rights leaders, ministers who lead protests, and people who use marijuana. In 1970 differences among educational levels were greater among postwar white cohorts than among the prewar on feelings toward black militants and toward radical students. In 1972 both groups of postwar whites were somewhat more polarized by level of education on their feelings toward policemen. And, in 1972 the relationship of level of education toward feelings toward women's liberation was stronger among the youngest white cohort than among the two older cohorts.

The greater polarization among the young might be a life-cycle phenomenon, and only data covering more time will allow us to test between a life-cycle and a generational explanation for these differences. But the greater polarization among younger whites may result from fundamental differences between the socialization of postwar cohorts and that of their elders. The technologically competent young, relatively free from pressing economic concerns, are more likely to sympathize with the demands of the functionally superfluous and are more tolerant of the counterculture. The less educated young, who are more likely to face economic hardships during periods of rapid technological change, more often support traditional norms. Regardless of which interpretation is valid, however, the data suggest no simple value conflict *between* generations, for age-group differences are concentrated among the relatively well educated. Moreover, there are basic value conflicts *within* generations, and these conflicts are often greater among the younger generations than among their elders.

Notes

1. See David E. Apter, *Choice and the Politics of Allocation: A Developmental Theory* (New Haven: Yale University Press, 1971), pp. 72-104. Also see, Apter, "Ideology and Discontent," in Apter, ed., *Ideology and Discontent* (New York: Free Press, 1964), pp. 15-46.

2. Walter Dean Burnham, *Critical Elections and the Mainsprings of American Politics* (New York: Norton, 1970), p. 141. Burnham's reformulation of Apter is based largely upon Apter's discussion in *Ideology and Discontent*.

3. Walter Dean Burnham, "Communication," *American Political Science Review*, 67 (June 1973): 569-74, at 570.

4. Ibid.

5. See "Perceptions of Presidential Candidates: Implications for Electoral Change," *Midwest Journal of Political Science*, 16 (August 1972): 388-410, at 399.

6. For a discussion of differing meanings of the generation gap, see Vern L. Bengtson, "The Generation Gap: A Review and Typology of Social-Psychological Perspectives," *Youth and Society*, 2 (September 1970): 7-32.

7. See Angus Campbell, *White Attitudes Toward Black People* (Ann Arbor, Michigan: Institute for Social Research, 1971), pp. 54-67; and Joel D. Aberbach and Jack L. Walker, *Race in the City: Political Trust and Public Policy in the New Urban System* (Boston: Little Brown, 1973), pp. 160-61.

8. Ronald Inglehart provides considerable evidence that European youths, especially those with high levels of education, tend to reject materialistic values and are more likely to have liberal attitudes than their elders. (See "The Silent Revolution: Intergenerational Change in Post-Industrial Societies," *American Political Science Review*, 65 [December 1971] : 991-1017.) Inglehart's reformulation of Abraham Maslow's psychological perspective is an important theoretical contribution, but as Inglehart used cross-sectional data he was unable to discriminate definitively between a life-cycle and generational explanation for his findings.

6 Attitudes, Feelings, and Partisanship

The attitudes and feelings we have examined related strongly to the way people voted for president in 1972. Although the candidates did not present the issues in the same terms used by the Michigan researchers, McGovern was far more disposed to helping minority groups than was Nixon. McGovern's pledge of $1,000 a year for each American was retracted quickly once it became clear that income redistribution might lead to higher taxes for his affluent supporters, but many Americans remembered the pledge and saw McGovern as a supporter of black demands. Although McGovern equivocated on many of the so-called style issues, he was viewed as sympathetic toward the counterculture. McGovern did not take a stand for law and order. He was not identified with symbols of authority, and, as a long-time opponent of the Vietnam War, was seen as hostile toward the military.

Nixon strongly supported law and order. While avoiding direct racist appeals, he benignly neglected black demands. After Wallace's success in the Florida primary, as well as the overwhelming support for an antibusing referendum, Nixon took a firm stand against busing as a means to achieve racial integration. He was openly hostile toward the counterculture, condemning campus protestors as bums and vigorously opposing amnesty for draft evaders. His opposition to abortion reform marked him as a foe of women's liberation.

The party conventions underscored the contrast between the candidates. Because of McGovern's reforms, the Democrats had introduced guidelines to assure a large representation of blacks, women, and youth. These guidelines, more often seen as quotas, did not affect the outcome of the nomination. The youngest, blackest, and most feminine convention in American history nominated a fifty-year-old white, Anglo-Saxon male on its first ballot. But the convention's tone was affected greatly by its social composition. The delegates' youth and casual dress highlighted their differences from previous delegations. Although the McGovern leadership tightly controlled their followers during the credential debates, they failed to prevent embarrassing platform debates from reaching the floor. We cannot prove that the convention itself influenced votes, but even in the hiatus between the convention's adjournment and the exposure of Eagleton's medical history, McGovern's popularity declined in the polls.[a]

---

[a]Goldwater, by contrast, rose in the polls after the 1964 Republican convention. That McGovern dropped strongly suggests that the convention cost him votes, but this cannot be demonstrated definitively without panel data. An analysis of the 1972 Michigan election survey by Arthur H. Miller and his colleagues suggests that the convention can account for only a small percentage of the total Democratic defections. See "A Majority Party in Disarray," pp. 41-42.

By contrast, the Republican convention was a staid and orchestrated meeting of well-dressed Middle Americans, which may have evoked, along with boredom, a feeling of confidence for its nominee. The Republicans appeared to be the party of order, committed to preserving the traditional norms of the middle stratum.

McGovern's defeat was staggering. Only one adult in five voted for him, as the data presented earlier in Table 1-1 show. How could the standard-bearer of a "majority party" fare so poorly? The answer is simple. Even among Democrats, McGovern did badly. Among white major-party voters, only 66 percent of the strong Democrats supported McGovern, while among weak Democrats only 44 percent did; among Independents who leaned Democratic, McGovern gained 58 percent. McGovern fared far worse among Democratic identifiers than Goldwater had fared among Republican identifiers eight years earlier.[b]

But the 1972 campaign was not just a popularity contest between two candidates, for the electorate was offered a clearer choice over issues than in most elections. Unfortunately for the Democrats, McGovern's position on the issues was less popular than Nixon's. The Michigan Center for Political Studies' 1972 survey clearly shows that Nixon was perceived to be far closer to the attitudes of most Americans than McGovern was.[1] Their study also shows that issues strongly influenced the way people voted.[2] And the issues and feelings we analyzed in Chapter 5 related closely to the way people voted for president.

Attitudes, Feelings, and Voting Behavior in 1972

Table 6-1 presents the basic relationship between attitudes and direction of presidential vote among whites, and Table 6-2 presents the relationship between feelings toward groups and presidential voting.[c] Whites who supported minority groups, were cool toward established authorities, and sympathetic to protestors and to the counterculture, were most strongly for McGovern. As Nixon received 70 percent of the white major-party vote, it is difficult to find groups of whites among whom a majority voted for McGovern. Yet, among white major-party voters who strongly favored[d] aiding minority groups, 55 percent voted for McGovern, and among those who strongly sympathized with student and faculty demonstrators, 64 percent did. Among whites who strongly favored solving the

---

[b]Among white major-party voters in 1964, 91 percent of the strong Republicans voted for Goldwater, 60 percent of the weak Republicans, and 75 percent of the Independents who leaned toward the Republican party.

[c]I have regrouped the feeling thermometer responses into a five-fold ordinal classification to present the percentage voting for McGovern in a readable manner. However, the relationships presented in Table 6-2 are the Pearson's r correlations based upon the entire range of responses on each thermometer item.

[d]Throughout this discussion the term "strongly favored" refers to scores of 1 and 2 on the seven-point policy scale. (See pp. 74-75 for a full description of these items.)

Table 6-1
Percentage of White Major-Party Voters Who Voted for McGovern in 1972, by Attitudes Toward Policy Questions

Self-Location on Policy Scale:	1	2	3	4	5	6	7	Relationship Between Attitudes and Direction of Presidential Vote[a]
Percentage for McGovern, by attitude toward minority groups: Government should help minority groups	55% (109)[b]	55% (92)	34% (189)	29% (341)	20% (157)	18% (171)	25% (233) Minority groups should help themselves	.21
Percentage for McGovern, by attitude toward urban unrest: Solve problems of poverty and unemployment	44% (174)	39% (88)	31% (78)	22% (110)	16% (50)	17% (29)	21% (84) Use all available force	.21
Percentage for McGovern, by attitude toward campus unrest: Sympathetic with students and faculty	65% (37)	62% (26)	54% (52)	30% (140)	26% (86)	17% (86)	20% (173) Use force to stop disturbances	.30

[a] Pearson's r correlation between a seven-fold measure of attitude as listed above and dichotomized direction of presidential vote.
[b] Numbers in parentheses are the totals upon which percentages are based.

Table 6-2
Percentage of White Major-Party Voters Who Voted for McGovern in 1972, by Feelings Toward Groups

Feeling Toward Group:	Less Than 30	30 Degrees to 49 Degrees	50 Degrees	51 Degrees to 69 Degrees	70 Degrees or More	Relationship Between Feeling Toward Group and Direction of Presidential Vote[a]
Percentage for McGovern, by feelings toward whites:	(0)	(1)[b] (4)	35% (208)	35% (90)	28% (1018)	−.06
Percentage for McGovern, by feelings toward the military:	78% (50)	58% (110)	32% (180)	29% (170)	22% (806)	−.25
Percentage for McGovern, by feelings toward policemen:	69% (13)	59% (41)	43% (90)	39% (155)	25% (1034)	−.18
Percentage for McGovern, by feelings toward black militants:	23% (942)	40% (240)	51% (75)	53% (30)	69% (16)	.24
Percentage for McGovern, by feelings toward people who riot in cities:	25% (1058)	42% (204)	55% (49)	82% (11)	(4)	.23
Percentage for McGovern, by feelings toward radical students:	21% (675)	30% (394)	46% (122)	55% (62)	63% (43)	.25
Percentage for McGovern, by feelings toward civil rights leaders:	23% (440)	21% (258)	28% (201)	31% (202)	56% (192)	.20
Percentage for McGovern, by feelings toward ministers who lead protest marches:	23% (524)	20% (291)	31% (223)	33% (121)	61% (155)	.22

Percentage for McGovern, by feelings toward blacks:	14%	(37)	19%	(136)	32%	(333)	24%	(292)	35%	(518)	.11
Percentage for McGovern, by feelings toward women's liberation movement:	22%	(294)	21%	(264)	27%	(276)	39%	(173)	41%	(287)	.16
Percentage for McGovern, by feelings toward people who use marijuana:	22%	(788)	28%	(243)	42%	(184)	39%	(28)	67%	(79)	.24

[a]Pearson's r correlation between scores on thermometer items and dichotomized direction of presidential vote. (Although the percentages are based upon a five-fold ordinal division, the correlations are based upon the entire range on the thermometer questions.)

[b]Numbers in parentheses are the totals upon which percentages are based.

problems of poverty to deal with urban unrest, 42 percent voted for McGovern, well above the mean for the white electorate.

Only two of the 11 items measuring feelings toward groups related weakly to direction of presidential vote—feelings toward whites and feelings toward blacks. On all other items, except feelings toward women's liberation, a majority of strongly liberal whites voted for McGovern. Among whites less than 50 degrees toward the military, 64 percent voted for McGovern, and among those less than 50 degrees toward policemen, 61 percent did. Among whites scoring over 50 degrees toward black militants, 59 percent voted for McGovern; among those over 50 degrees toward people who riot in cities, 68 percent did, and among whites over 50 degrees toward radical students, 58 percent voted Democratic. Among white voters who felt 70 degrees or warmer toward civil rights leaders, 56 percent voted for McGovern; among those 70 degrees or more toward ministers who lead protest marches, 61 percent did, and among whites who felt 70 degrees or warmer toward marijuana users, 67 percent voted Democratic. Those groups that gave a majority of their vote to McGovern were always relatively small.

We would expect relationships between attitudes and feelings and direction of presidential vote to be stronger among young voters than among their elders, for the young should be affected more than their elders by issues that arose during the last decade. Moreover, the relationship between attitudes and voting should be stronger among the better educated, for they should be more aware of the issue positions of the candidates and parties, and more likely to vote according to those issues. Table 6-3 presents the relationship between attitudes and direction of presidential vote among different educational levels among three age cohorts, and Table 6-4 presents the relationship between feelings and direction of presidential vote by level of education and age.[e] Because the correlations show the relationship between attitudes and vote among fairly small subsets, and, as the Ns upon which these correlations are based are not presented,[f] I have noted those cases where the direction of the relationship is unlikely to have occurred by chance. What concerns us is not any single relationship, however, but the pattern of relationships in both these tables.

The data support our expectation that the young will be more influenced by their attitudes than will their elders. For all three policy questions, attitude differences relate more strongly to the direction of presidential vote among voters born in 1940 and after than among the prewar cohort. For nine of the 11 thermometer questions, the relationship between feelings and direction of presidential vote was stronger among the cohort born in 1940 and after than

---

[e]For the first three items I show the correlation between "coolness" toward the group and support for McGovern. Thus, the direction of the relationship has been reversed from that presented in Table 6-2.

[f]However, one may approximate the size of each subset by referring to the frequency distributions presented in Table 5-2.

Table 6-3
Relationship[a] Between Attitudes and Direction of Presidential Vote Among Whites in 1972, by Level of Education and Years of Birth[b]

Level of Education:	Eight Grades or Less	Some High School	High School Graduate	Some College	College Graduate	Relationship Among Age Group
Relationship between attitudes toward aiding minority groups and direction of presidential vote, by years of birth:						
Before 1924	.19*	.19*	.13	.13	.43***	.18***
1924-1939	.12	-.02	.23**	.21*	.34***	.21***
1940-1954	†	.06	.08	.27***	.29**	.21***
Relationship between attitudes toward urban unrest and direction of presidential vote, by years of birth:[c]						
Before 1924	.27	.29*	.07	.12	.10	.18**
1924-1939	†	.40	.00	.08	.14	.06
1940-1954	†	.34	.26*	.35**	.33*	.33***
Relationship between attitudes toward student and faculty demonstrators and direction of presidential vote, by years of birth:[c]						
Before 1924	.14	.36**	.10	.21	.36*	.19**
1924-1939	†	.24	.37***	.31*	.52***	.33***
1940-1954	†	.14	-.15	.46***	.58***	.33***

[a]Pearson's r correlation between a seven-fold measure of attitude as shown in Table 6-1 and dichotomized direction of presidential vote.
[b]To approximate the size of each subset, see Table 5-2.
[c]These items were asked of only one half the sample.
 *$P =$ or $< .05$
 **$P =$ or $< .01$
 ***$P =$ or $< .001$
†Because of the small Ns, the relationship has not been presented.

Table 6-4
Relationship[a] Between Feelings Toward Groups and Direction of Presidential Vote Among Whites in 1972, by Level of Education and Years of Birth[b]

Level of Education:	Eight Grades or Less	Some High School	High School Graduate	Some College	College Graduate	Relationship Among Age Group
Coolness toward whites and support for McGovern, by years of birth:						
Before 1924	−.05	.01	.02	.01	.04	−.02
1924-1939	.01	−.15	.06	.12	.23*	.09*
1940-1954	†	−.19	−.02	.10	−.07	.03
Coolness toward the military and support for McGovern, by years of birth:						
Before 1924	.02	.07	.05	.22*	.34**	.08*
1924-1939	.24	.06	.24**	.35**	.43***	.27***
1940-1954	†	.25	.15*	.38***	.42***	.31***
Coolness toward policemen and support for McGovern, by years of birth:						
Berore 1924	−.12	−.02	.20***	−.13	.31*	.04
1924-1939	.25	−.02	.12	.13	.29**	.15**
1940-1954	†	.10	.21**	.30***	.34***	.27***
Warmth toward black militants and support for McGovern, by years of birth:						
Before 1924	−.03	.29**	−.01	.20	.34**	.10*
1924-1939	.50**	−.07	.28***	.31**	.34***	.28***
1940-1954	†	−.07	.16*	.35***	.47***	.28***

Warmth toward people who riot in cities and support for McGovern, by years of birth:					
Before 1924	−.02	.14	.06	.22	.22*	.08*
1924-1939	.35	−.07	.10	.24*	.40***	.20***
1940-1954	†	.11	.13	.41***	.47***	.31***
Warmth toward radical students and support for McGovern, by years of birth:					
Before 1924	.11	.29**	−.05	.18	.10	.11**
1924-1939	.24	−.14	.20**	.36***	.43***	.25***
1940-1954	†	.01	.17*	.39***	.56***	.33***
Warmth toward civil rights leaders and support for McGovern, by years of birth:					
Before 1924	.15*	.16*	−.06	.15	.35**	.10*
1924-1939	.20	−.04	.15*	.22*	.42***	.19***
1940-1954	†	−.17	.03	.31***	.51***	.23***
Warmth toward ministers who lead protest marches and support for McGovern, by years of birth:					
Before 1924	.07	.19**	−.01	.01	.25*	.07*
1924-1939	.28	−.04	.24**	.35***	.45***	.26***
1940-1954	†	.06	−.01	.34***	.55***	.25***
Warmth toward blacks and support for McGovern, by years of birth:					
Before 1924	.14*	.00	.08	.06	.13	.08*
1924-1939	.23	.37**	.10	.02	.15	.12**
1940-1954	†	.14	.06	.19*	.34***	.17***

Table 6-4 (cont.)

Level of Education:	Eight Grades or Less	Some High School	High School Graduate	Some College	College Graduate	Relationship Among Age Group
Warmth toward women's liberation movement and support for McGovern, by years of birth:						
Before 1924	.14	.16	.01	.38**	.30*	.14***
1924-1939	−.07	.28*	.16*	.22*	.33***	.15**
1940-1954	†	.23	−.09	.23**	.37***	.16***
Warmth toward people who use marijuana and support for McGovern, by years of birth:						
Before 1924	.05	.04	.10	.25*	.28*	.09*
1924-1939	−.02	.01	.21**	.39***	.29***	.22***
1940-1954	†	.20	.18*	.28***	.46***	.29***

aPearson's r correlation between scores on thermometer items and dichotomized direction of presidential vote.
bTo approximate the size of each subset, see Table 5-2.
*P = or < .05
**P = or < .01
***P = or < .001
†Because of small Ns, the relationship has not been presented.

among the prewar age group, and for seven of these questions the relationship was stronger among the youngest cohort than among the age group born between 1924 and 1939. Members of the 1924 to 1939 cohort were usually more influenced by their attitudes than the prewar cohort. On two of the three policy items, the 1924 to 1939 cohort was more strongly influenced by their attitudes than the prewar cohort, although the prewar cohort was influenced more by its attitudes toward urban unrest. But the relationship between feelings toward groups and direction of presidential vote among the 1924 to 1939 cohort was stronger than among their elders on 10 of the 11 thermometer items.

Our second expectation was also supported. Attitudes and feelings related more strongly to voting among the better educated. The greater influence of attitudes and feelings upon the behavior of the young, therefore, partly results from their higher levels of education. But among persons with at least some college education the tendency of the young to be more influenced by their attitudes persisted even after controls for education were introduced.

College graduates born in 1940 and after were the most polarized in their voting by their attitudes toward campus unrest, and among the most polarized by their attitudes toward minority group aid and urban unrest. These young college graduates were strongly polarized by their feelings on all thermometer items, except feelings toward whites. On seven of the 11 items they were more polarized than any other subset, and in three cases they were the second most polarized group. Put differently, young college graduates who were liberal were very heavily for McGovern, while conservatives were heavily for Nixon. Young whites with some college education also were polarized strongly by their attitudes and feelings, the liberals being much more likely to vote for McGovern than the conservatives. College graduates born between 1924 and 1939 were also among the most polarized subsets of the electorate. And although whites with some college education born between 1924 and 1939 were not as polarized as college graduates, they, too, were often strongly affected by their attitudes and feelings.

Does the polarization among the young college educated presage growing polarization among the entire electorate? This question cannot be answered, for we know little about attitude formation during periods of partisan change. But even if the polarization of the highly-educated young does not presage a trend, that polarization is important. Although the young college educated make up only a small percentage of the electorate, their influence may be greater than their numbers. Given Democratic rules, which weaken the power of elected officials, young college graduates with organizational skills and leisure may be disproportionately influential in selecting presidential nominees.

Attitudes, Feelings, and Party Identification in 1970 and 1972

Some would argue that attitudes cannot contribute to new partisan alignments unless they influence party identification. But the attitudes and feelings I have examined virtually are unrelated to direction of party identification.[3] In 1970, for example, the highest relationship between attitude preference and party identification among whites was a modest .10 between tending toward government aid for minority groups and identifying as Democratic, and the highest positive correlation between feelings toward a group and party identification was .09 between warmth toward ministers who lead protests and Democratic identification.[g] In 1972 the highest relationship between attitude preferences and partisanship was .14 between sympathizing with student and faculty demonstrators and identifying as a Democrat, and the highest correlation between feelings and party identification was .10 between warmth toward women's liberation and support for the Democratic party. One might expect higher relationships among the young who may be influenced more strongly by issues contributing to new partisan alignments, but even among the young there were only modest relationships between attitudes and feelings and direction of party identification.

Although these attitudes and feelings were related weakly to party identification among the white electorate as a whole, there was often a strong relationship among college graduates, especially among graduates born in 1940 and after. The relationships of policy attitudes toward party identification among whites of differing educational levels within each cohort are presented in Tables 6-5 and 6-6, and the relationship of feelings to identification among these subgroups is presented in Tables 6-7 and 6-8. Once again I have indicated those cases where the direction of the relationship was unlikely to have occurred by chance.[h]

We are interested primarily in the relationship between attitudes, feelings, and direction of partisanship among the young college-educated, and it is useful to point out those cases where the same relationship occurred in both 1970 and 1972. In both years there was a strong tendency for the college graduates born in 1940 and after who favored aiding minority groups to identify as Democrats; in both years those who sympathized with student and faculty demonstrators were more Democratic than those who favored force to end campus unrest. In both years young college graduates who were relatively cool toward the military and toward policemen were more likely to identify as Democrats than those who were warm toward those symbols of authority. Moreover, in both years young graduates who were relatively warm toward black militants, radical students, civil rights leaders, ministers who lead protests, blacks, and marijuana users were more likely to identify as Democrats than those who were cool toward those groups.

There was often a strong relationship between these attitudes and feelings and direction of party identification among college graduates born between 1924

---

[g]However, persons who were warm toward whites were more likely to identify as Democrats, and this correlation was .10. But our basic thesis suggests that persons supporting established authorities should be less likely to be Democratic.

[h]The Ns for each subset can be approximated by referring to Tables 5-1 and 5-2.

115

Warmth toward Negroes and support for Democratic party, by years of birth:						
Before 1924	−.08	.08	.03	.03	.27*	−.03
1924-1939	.00	.25*	−.02	.09	.40***	.05
1940-1952	†	.12	.05	−.03	.27*	.07
Warmth toward women's liberation movement and support for Democratic party, by years of birth:						
Before 1924	.09	−.08	.08	.33*	.18	.10**
1924-1939	−.34*	.15	−.03	.28*	.22	.04
1940-1952	†	.04	.01	−.06	.13	.02
Warmth toward people who use marijuana and support for Democratic party, by years of birth:						
Before 1924	.06	−.04	−.08	.26*	.16	.00
1924-1939	.05	.10	.08	−.15	.44***	.04
1940-1952	†	−.19	−.02	.08	.35**	.05

aPearson's r correlation between scores on thermometer items and seven-fold measure of party identification described in Chapter 4.
bTo approximate the size of each subset, see Table 5-1.
*P = or < .05
**P = or < .01
***P = or < .001
†Because of small Ns, the relationship has not been presented.

Table 6-8
Relationship[a] Between Feelings Toward Groups and Direction of Party Identification Among Whites in 1972, by Level of Education and Years of Birth[b]

Level of Education:	Eight Grades or Less	Some High School	High School Graduate	Some College	College Graduate	Relationship Among Age Group
Coolness toward whites and support for Democratic party, by years of birth:						
Before 1924	-.11*	-.07	-.03	-.13	-.02	-.10**
1924-1939	-.11	-.06	-.08	.18*	.06	-.04
1940-1954	.29	-.12	-.03	-.17*	.04	-.06
Coolness toward the military and support for Democratic party, by years of birth:						
Before 1924	.01	.03	-.09	-.08	.08	-.04
1924-1939	-.24	.15	-.01	.22*	.21*	.04
1940-1954	.09	.10	.03	.09	.30***	.09*
Coolness toward policemen and support for Democratic party, by years of birth:						
Before 1924	-.11*	-.05	.03	-.10	.23*	-.05
1924-1939	-.13	.07	.05	.25**	.04	.04
1940-1954	.16	-.13	.01	.05	.25**	.05
Warmth toward black militants and support for Democratic party, by years of birth:						
Before 1924	.04	.08	.10	.12	.06	.07*
1924-1939	.08	-.02	.05	.13	.16*	.05
1940-1954	.01	.07	.08	.16*	.33***	.13***

Warmth toward people who riot in cities and support for Democratic party, by years of birth:						
Before 1924	.08	−.02	.09	.15	.09	.06*
1924-1939	−.07	−.16	.04	.20*	.23**	.05
1940-1954	−.06	.12	.00	.30***	.32***	.15***
Warmth toward radical students and support for Democratic party, by years of birth:						
Before 1924	.11*	.22**	.13*	.12	.01	.13***
1924-1939	−.06	−.04	.04	.16	.16	.05
1940-1954	.07	.13	.02	.25***	.42***	.17***
Warmth toward civil rights leaders and support for Democratic party, by years of birth:						
Before 1924	.18**	.07	−.03	.19	.21*	.07*
1924-1939	.36**	−.19	.01	.24*	.29**	.04
1940-1954	.20	−.10	.00	.16*	.29***	.07
Warmth toward ministers who lead protest marches and support for Democratic party, by years of birth:						
Before 1924	.17**	.02	.06	.05	.09	.06*
1924-1939	.20	.05	.01	.16	.32***	.06
1940-1954	.06	−.06	.07	.18*	.34***	.11**
Warmth toward blacks and support for Democratic party, by years of birth:						
Before 1924	.10	−.02	.09	.09	.04	.05
1924-1939	.01	.17	.05	−.10	.03	.02
1940-1954	.02	.06	.11	.19**	.18*	.12***

Table 6-8 (cont.)

Level of Education:	Eight Grades or Less	Some High School	High School Graduate	Some College	College Graduate	Relationship Among Age Group
Warmth toward women's liberation movement and support for Democratic party, by years of birth:						
Before 1924	.23***	−.02	.05	.11	.24	.12***
1924-1939	.27*	−.16	.05	.05	.34***	.09*
1940-1954	−.10	.17	−.02	.17*	.28**	.08*
Warmth toward people who use marijuana and support for Democratic party, by years of birth:						
Before 1924	.07	.04	.02	−.03	.13	.01
1924-1939	−.12	−.14	.13*	.28**	.10	.04
1940-1954	.17	−.04	.05	.07	.38***	.08*

aPearson's *r* correlations between scores on thermometer items and seven-fold measure of party identification described in Chapter 4.
bTo approximate the size of each subset, see Table 5-2.

*P = or < .05
**P = or < .01
***P = or < .001

and 1939, although these relationships were not as consistent as those among the younger college graduates. In both 1970 and 1972 college graduates born between 1924 and 1939 who tended to support government aid for minority groups were more likely to identify as Democrats than those who said minority groups should help themselves. In both years college graduates in this cohort who were relatively cool toward the military were more likely to identify as Democrats than those who were warm. In both years college graduates of this age group who were relatively warm toward black militants, urban rioters, civil rights leaders, and ministers who lead protests were more likely to identify as Democrats than those who were relatively cool toward those groups. Among older college graduates, however, there was less often a tendency for the more liberal to identify as Democrats.

Viewed differently, these data show that young, white college-educated Democrats were far more liberal than the white electorate as a whole. In 1970, 72 percent of the Democratic and Democratic-leaning[i] college graduates born in 1940 and after ($n = 25$)[j] tended to favor government aid for minority groups and 64 percent sympathized with student and faculty demonstrators. In 1972, 69 percent of the young Democratic college graduates ($n = 51$) favored government aid to minority groups and 59 percent sympathized with student and faculty demonstrators. These young Democratic graduates had attitudes sharply different from those held by post whites (see pp. 76-77), and as overall attitudes of white Democrats differed little from those of whites as a whole, these young Democratic graduates had views that set them apart from most other Democrats.

Young Democratic college graduates were cooler toward symbols of authority than the overall population (see Tables 5-6 and 5-7 for the overall feelings of whites) and, as the overall feelings of white Democrats were similar to those of whites as a whole, the young Democratic graduates had feelings markedly different from those of most other Democrats. In 1970 young Democratic graduates averaged only 33 degrees toward the military and 65 degrees toward policemen; in 1972 the mean score of young Democratic graduates toward the military was 40 degrees, while they averaged 60 degrees toward policemen. In addition, young Democratic college graduates were much more supportive of protestors, groups symbolizing the counterculture, and black leaders than was the white population as a whole (and more than most other white Democrats). In 1970 these young Democrats averaged 30 degrees toward black militants, 37 degrees toward radical students, 68 degrees toward civil rights leaders, 61 degrees toward ministers who lead protest marches, and 46 degrees toward marijuana users. These warm feelings persisted in 1972. Young Democratic graduates

---

[i]Among these young college graduates, Democratic leaners usually had attitudes similar to Democratic identifiers; Republican leaners had attitudes similar to Republican identifiers.

[j]Here and in subsequent reports I show the total number of partisans within each age group. The actual N upon which the percentages and mean scores are based will vary from item to item. Numbers for 1972 include only those partisans in the post-election interview.

scored 35 degrees toward black militants, 46 degrees toward radical students, 67 degrees toward civil rights leaders, 65 degrees toward ministers who lead protests, and 56 degrees toward marijuana users.

Democratic and Democratic-leaning college graduates born between 1924 and 1939[k] were not as liberal as the younger Democratic graduates, but they, too, usually held attitudes and feelings far more liberal than those of the white population as a whole, and of most other white Democrats. One may examine those items on which this cohort of college graduates was polarized by direction of party identification in both surveys. In 1972, 67 percent of the Democratic college graduates born between 1924 and 1939 ($n = 27$) favored government aid for minority groups; in 1972, 46 percent of the Democratic college graduates in this cohort ($n = 36$) favored government aid for minorities. In both years these Democratic graduates were relatively cool toward the military. In 1970 they felt 53 degrees toward the military; in 1972 they averaged 57 degrees. In both years these Democratic graduates were relatively warm toward groups who made blacks' demands. In 1970 they averaged 34 degrees toward black militants, 17 degrees toward urban rioters, 60 degrees toward civil rights leaders, and 54 degrees toward ministers who lead protest marches. In 1972 the Democratic graduates in this age group averaged 21 degrees toward black militants, 20 degrees toward urban rioters, 55 degrees toward civil rights leaders, and 51 degrees toward ministers who lead protest marches.

By isolating relationships among the subset of young college graduates we point to potential problems for the Democratic party. Admittedly there are few postwar college graduates. Even in 1972 only nine percent of the electorate were white college graduates born after 1923, and only five percent of the Democratic party identifiers were white graduates who entered the electorate after World War II.[l] (White college graduates born in 1940 and after made up only five percent of the electorate and three percent of the Democratic identifiers.[m]) These young graduates, even combined with blacks, cannot form a winning electoral coalition. But postwar college graduates may disproportionately influence the presidential nominating process. In 1972 young college graduates, who often supported McGovern, were able to exert considerable influence, partly because McGovern's supporters better understood the new Democratic party rules. The party regulars and the Wallace supporters were caught flat-footed. In some states, New York being the most important, a small number of McGovern supporters were able to capture entire delegations. A take-over by Leftist activists is unlikely to recur. Moreover, rules encouraging proportional repre-

[k]Among these graduates, Democratic leaners usually had attitudes similar to Democratic identifiers; Republican leaners had attitudes similar to Republican identifiers.

[l]Based upon strong and weak Democrats. If we include Independents who lean toward the Democrats, seven percent were white college graduates born in 1924 and after.

[m]If we include Independents who lean toward the Democrats, four percent were white college graduates born in 1940 and after.

sentation for candidates according to primary results will weaken the ability of activists to influence delegate selection.

In spite of new circumstances and new rules, the college-educated young may still exert more than their share of influence, for they have the organizational skills and leisure to compete in the struggle over delegates. And if these data are correct, young Democratic graduates differ markedly not only from the white population as a whole, but from most other white Democrats. Depending upon their commitment and involvement, they may obstruct a Democratic move to the political center. And if the Democrats do move to the center and nominate a candidate unacceptable to the young college educated, they may provide the cadre for a third party of the Left. Regardless which scenario proves correct, these data show that the Democrats are deeply divided. The most articulate Democrats, who could provide a leadership corps, are greatly at odds with their potential followers.

Notes

1. See Arthur H. Miller, et al., "A Majority Party in Disarray: Policy Polarization in the 1972 Election," paper presented at the 69th annual meeting of the American Political Science Association, New Orleans, September, 1973, pp. 16-17.

2. Ibid., passim.

3. Jerrold G. Rusk and Herbert F. Weisberg also reported that these attitudes were related only weakly to direction of party identification in 1970. (See "Perceptions of Presidential Candidates: Implications for Electoral Change," *Midwest Journal of Political Science*, 16 [August 1972] : 399-400.) See also Teresa E. Levitin and Warren E. Miller, "The New Politics and Partisan Realignment," paper presented to the 68th Annual Meeting of the American Political Science Association, Washington, D.C. 1972, pp. 23-25. Arthur H. Miller and his colleagues also reported that relationships between these policy attitudes and party identification were weak in 1972, but note that policy attitudes and direction of party identification were correlated more highly among the young and better educated than among other demographic groups. (See "A Majority Party in Disarray," p. 72.)

7 Conclusions

This study demonstrated some basic trends in American politics, and by studying age-group differences, it shed light on the processes through which they occurred. We began by documenting the declining relationship between social class and presidential voting, a decline which, along with the mass mobilization of blacks into the electorate, transformed the social composition of the Democratic presidential coalition. The trend toward declining class voting was not perfectly consistent, for class voting rose in 1964; but we gained greater confidence about the direction of that trend through a time-series cohort analysis. By testing between alternative explanations for age-group differences we showed that low levels of class voting among the postwar electorate did not result from their youth, but from generational differences between their formative socialization and that of their elders. Persons who entered the electorate after the war had formative socialization experiences contributing to a weak relationship between class and party choice, and they are likely to continue to have low levels of class voting as they age. Moreover, the overall decline in class voting, at least through 1968, largely resulted from postwar voters entering the electorate. Thus, we were able to examine a process through which partisan alignments are transformed, namely through generational change in which the relationships of social characteristics to voting behavior among older generations tend to persist, although older generations gradually are replaced by newer generations among whom different relationships prevail.

The decline in partisan loyalties among white Americans since 1964 is an even clearer trend, for that erosion has continued consistently. That decline, too, resulted from generational change. It was well known that young adults had weaker party identifications than their elders, but it usually was argued that their weak partisanship resulted from their political inexperience—as they aged they would become more partisan. Indeed, the authors of *The American Voter* advanced a plausible life-cycle explanation for the weak partisanship of young adults, and provided some evidence for their interpretation. Yet, a time-series cohort analysis demonstrates conclusively that young adults did not become more partisan as they aged, and it provides considerable support for a generational interpretation for the weak party identifications of young Americans. Moreover, the overall decline in party identifications among white Americans results almost entirely from persons born in 1924 and after entering the electorate. Once again we gained insight into an important change process, for the decline in party identification was caused by the transformation of the electorate. High levels of partisan identification persisted among older generations, although gradually they have been replaced by new generations with weak partisan feelings.

Our analysis of political attitudes and feelings can only hint at possible trends. There is some basis for projecting growing attitudinal similarity between upper-stratum whites and blacks, for the postwar college-educated whites are more like blacks in their attitudes and feelings than are their comparably educated elders. And there is some evidence that attitudinal polarization is greater among younger generations of whites than among their elders. The attitudes and feelings we examined related strongly to the way whites voted for president in 1972, especially among the young college educated. These attitudes and feelings related only weakly to direction of party identification, but among the young college educated there was often a strong tendency for whites with liberal attitudes and feelings to identify as Democrats. The high level of polarization among the college-educated young may not presage trends among the electorate as a whole, but focusing on the attitudes of these educated youth demonstrated that the Democrats are deeply divided, and pointed to problems they may face in rebuilding a winning presidential coalition. We must be cautious, however, in projecting trends from our analysis of attitudes and feelings, for that analysis was based upon only two surveys. Only when data are collected over several decades can we discriminate adequately between a life-cycle and a generational explanation for age-group differences.

But even when we have data collected over many years, we should be cautious about predictions. Again, we may repeat Duncan's admonition: "There is nothing about a trend—supposing it to have been reliably ascertained for some specific period—that guarantees its own continuation." Cohort analysis, as Duncan recognizes, is one method for social forecasting, and it greatly helps to identify the processes through which some attitude changes occur. But social, economic, and political conditions that contributed to a trend may change. Changed economic conditions, for example, problems caused by world-wide scarcity, might make economic issues more salient and increase the importance of class upon partisan choice. Moreover, our analysis suggests that political leaders can affect class voting. Party leaders do not merely react to social change, they also create it. To some extent at least, the policies and programs espoused by party leaders will affect the relationship of social class to partisan choice. And if, as we have argued, the decline of party identification results largely from political conditions, that decline might be stopped or reversed if political leaders reemphasized partisan appeals. Moreover, future social and economic conditions might reduce the importance of the race-related issues that divide the electorate. If urban riots do not recur, middle-stratum whites may feel less threatened by black demands. If economic conditions deteriorate, economic issues might overshadow the race-related issues that divided the electorate in 1972, and the attitude differences that divide Democratic party identifiers might become less salient. Moreover, most important race-related reforms have been initiated by the courts, not by elected political leaders. If the courts cease to press for racial integration, some explosive racial issues, such as busing, may be defused. No analysis of currently available survey data can tell us how the future will unfold. Cohort analysis is a tool that helps us understand some change processes. It does not transform social scientists into seers.

Cohort analysis is a technique, not a substitute for theory. The vast pools of currently available survey data create great opportunities for cohort analysis, but such analysis will seldom lead to interesting results if it is merely a procedure to search atheoretically for possible age-group differences. We are likely to find consistent age-group differences only when we begin by examining attitudes that, on theoretical grounds, should be affected either by a person's position in the life cycle or by some major events that might affect the formative socialization of specified age groups. One of the virtues of *The American Voter* is that the authors advanced theoretically interesting explanations for age-group differences, and that they conducted preliminary tests between alternative explanations. Although I found a generational explanation better than the life-cycle explanation they advanced to account for the weak party identification of young adults, there may be cases where a generational explanation would be wrong. In our view, generational change explains age-group differences only for relatively stable attitudes. Only when we are examining such attitudes will generational change be an important process in explaining transformations among the electorate, for when attitudes are highly malleable, change will occur among all age groups. But even if many cohort analyses reject the generational explanation, social science will be served. It is important to identify age-group differences that result from life-cycle effects, those that result from both generational and life-cycle effects, as well as to discover attitudes that are not related systematically to age. Only when we can specify what types of attitude transformations occur through generational change, and what types occur through changes among all age groups, will we be able to develop more comprehensive theories of attitude change.

We have maintained in this book that generational change can be an important process in explaining social change, and have demonstrated several important trends that can be explained by the gradual transformation of the electorate. We have helped formulate the assumptions that constitute a generational explanation for age-group differences, and have specified procedures through which that explanation can be tested. Further research, especially cross-national research that allows us to discriminate between alternative explanations, is necessary before we can better understand attitudinal continuity and change among mass electorates.

Bibliography

Bibliography

Aberbach, Joel D. and Walker, Jack L. *Race in the City: Political Trust and Public Policy in the New Urban System*. Boston, Little Brown, 1973.

Abramson, Paul R. "Generational Change and Continuity in British Partisan Choice." Paper presented to the IXth World Congress of the International Political Science Association, Montreal, Canada, 1973.

_____. "Generational Change in American Electoral Behavior." *American Political Science Review* 68, 1974, pp. 93-105.

_____. "Social Class and Political Change in Western Europe: A Cross-National Longitudinal Analysis." *Comparative Political Studies* 4, 1971, pp. 131-155.

Alford, Robert R. "Class Voting in the Anglo-American Political Systems," in Seymour Martin Lipset and Stein Rokkan, eds. *Party Systems and Voter Alignments: Cross-National Perspectives*. New York: Free Press, 1967.

_____. *Party and Society: The Anglo-American Democracies*. Chicago: Rand McNally, 1963.

Apter, David E. *Choice and the Politics of Allocation: A Developmental Theory*. New Haven: Yale University Press, 1971.

_____. Ideology and Discontent," in David E. Apter, ed. *Ideology and Discontent*. New York: Free Press, 1964.

_____. "Radicalization and Embourgeoisement: Hypotheses for a Comparative Study of History." *Journal of Interdisciplinary History* 1, 1971, pp. 265-303.

Axelrod, Robert. "Where the Votes Come From: An Analysis of Electoral Coalitions, 1952-1968." *American Political Science Review* 66, 1972, pp. 11-20.

Beck, Paul Allen. "Partisan Stability and Change in the American South: 1952-1972." Paper presented to the 70th Annual Meeting of the American Political Science Association, Chicago, 1974.

Bell, Daniel. *The Coming of Post-Industrial Society: A Venture in Social Forecasting*. New York: Basic Books, 1973.

Bengtson, Vern L. "The Generation Gap: A Review and Typology of Social-Psychological Perspectives." *Youth and Society* 2, 1970, pp. 7-32.

Berelson, Bernard R.; Lazarsfeld, Paul F.; and McPhee, William N. *Voting: A Study of Opinion Formation in a Presidential Campaign*. Chicago: University of Chicago Press, 1954.

Blau, Peter M. and Duncan, Otis Dudley. *The American Occupational Structure*. New York: Wiley, 1967.

Broder, David S. *The Party's Over: The Failure of Politics in America*. New York: Harper and Row, 1972.

Burnham, Walter Dean. "The Changing Shape of the American Political Universe." *American Political Science Review* 59, 1965, pp. 7-28.

Burnham, Walter Dean. "Communication." *American Political Science Review* 67, 1973, pp. 569-74.

———. *Critical Elections and the Mainsprings of American Politics.* New York: Norton, 1970.

———. "The End of American Party Politics." *Trans-action* 7, 1969, pp. 12-22.

Butler, David and Stokes, Donald. *Political Change in Britain: Forces Shaping Electoral Choice.* New York: St. Martin's, 1969.

———. *Political Change in Britain: Forces Shaping Electoral Choice.* 2d ed. New York: St. Martin's, 1974.

Campbell, Angus. *White Attitudes Toward Black People.* Ann Arbor, Michigan: Institute for Social Research, 1971.

———, Converse, Philip E.; Miller, Warren E.; and Stokes, Donald E. *The American Voter.* New York: Wiley, 1960.

———, Converse, Philip E.; Miller, Warren E.; and Stokes, Donald E. *Elections and the Political Order.* New York: Wiley, 1966.

Converse, Philip E. "Change in the American Electorate," in Angus Campbell and Philip E. Converse, eds. *The Human Meaning of Social Change.* New York: Russell Sage, 1972.

———. "Of Time and Partisan Stability." *Comparative Political Studies* 2, 1969, pp. 139-71.

———. "On the Possibility of Major Political Realignment in the South," in Angus Campbell, Warren E. Miller, Philip E. Converse, and Donald E. Stokes, *Elections and the Political Order.* New York: Wiley, 1966.

Cutler, Neal E. *The Alternative Effects of Generations and Aging Upon Political Behavior: A Cohort Analysis of American Attitudes Toward Foreign Policy, 1946-1966.* Oak Ridge, Tennessee: Oak Ridge National Laboratory, 1968.

Dreyer, Edward C. "Change and Stability in Party Identifications." *Journal of Politics* 35, 1973, pp. 712-22.

Duncan, Otis Dudley. "Social Forecasting—The State of the Art." *The Public Interest* 17, 1969, pp. 88-118.

———. "Social Stratification and Mobility: Problems in the Measurement of a Trend," in Eleanor B. Sheldon and Wilbert E. Moore, eds. *Indicators of Social Change: Concepts and Measurement.* New York: Russell Sage, 1968.

Eulau, Heinz. *Class and Party in the Eisenhower Years: Class Roles and Perspectives in the 1952 and 1956 Elections.* New York: Free Press, 1962.

The Freedom to Vote Task Force, Democratic National Committee. *That All May Vote.* December 16, 1969.

Glenn, Norval D. "Class and Party Support in 1972." mimeo, 1973.

———. "Class and Party Support in the United States: Recent and Emerging Trends." *Public Opinion Quarterly* 37, 1973, pp. 1-20.

———. "Sources of Shift to Political Independence: Some Evidence from a Cohort Analysis." *Social Science Quarterly* 53, 1972, pp. 494-519.

_____ and Hefner, Ted. "Further Evidence on Aging and Party Identification." *Public Opinion Quarterly* 36, 1972, pp. 31-47.
Hamilton, Richard F. *Class and Politics in the United States*. New York: Wiley, 1972.
Hyman, Herbert H. *Secondary Analysis of Sample Surveys: Principles, Procedures and Potentialities*. New York: Wiley, 1972.
Inglehart, Ronald. "The Silent Revolution in Europe: Intergenerational Change in Post-Industrial Societies." *American Political Science Review* 65, 1971, pp. 991-1017.
_____ and Hochstein, Avram. "Alignment and Dealignment of the Electorate in France and the United States." *Comparative Political Studies* 5, 1972, pp. 343-72.
Jencks, Christopher. *Inequality: A Reassessment of the Effects of Family and Schooling in America*. New York: Basic Books, 1972.
Jennings, M. Kent and Niemi, Richard G. "Continuity and Change in Political Orientations: A Longitudinal Study of Two Generations." Paper presented to the 69th Annual Meeting of the American Political Science Association, New Orleans, 1973.
Key, V.O., Jr. *Southern Politics in State and Nation*. New York: Knopf, 1949.
Kolko, Gabriel. *Wealth and Power in America*. New York: Praeger, 1962.
Korpi, Walter. "Some Problems in the Measurement of Class Voting." *American Journal of Sociology* 78, 1972, pp. 627-42.
Levitin, Teresa E. and Miller, Warren E. "The New Politics and Partisan Realignment." Paper presented to the 68th Annual Meeting of the American Political Science Association, Washington, D.C. 1972.
Leuchtenburg, William E. *Franklin D. Roosevelt and the New Deal: 1932-1940*. New York: Harper and Row, 1963.
Lipset, Seymour Martin and Rabb, Earl. *The Politics of Unreason: Right-Wing Extremism in America, 1790-1970*. New York: Harper and Row, 1970.
Lubell, Samuel. *The Future of American Politics*. Garden City, N.Y.: Doubleday, 1956.
Mason, Karen Oppenheim; Mason, William M.; Winsborough, H.H.; and Poole, W. Kenneth. "Some Methodological Issues in Cohort Analysis of Archival Data." *American Sociological Review* 38, 1973, pp. 242-58.
Matthews, Donald R. and Prothro, James W. *Negroes and the New Southern Politics*. New York: Harcourt, Brace, and World, 1966.
McPhee, William N. and Ferguson, Jack. "Political Immunization," in William N. McPhee and William A. Glaser, eds. *Public Opinion and Congressional Elections*. New York: Free Press, 1962.
Miller, Arthur H.; Miller, Warren E.; Raine, Alden S.; and Brown, Thad A. "A Majority Party in Disarray: Policy Polarization in the 1972 Election." Paper presented at the 69th Annual Meeting of the American Political Science Association, New Orleans, 1973.

Miller, Herman P. *Income Distribution in the United States*. U.S. Bureau of the Census, A 1960 Census Monograph. Washington, D.C.: U.S. Government Printing Office, 1960.

Mosteller, Frederick; Hyman, Herbert; McCarthy, Philip J.; Marks, Eli S.; and Truman, David B. *The Pre-Election Polls of 1948: Report to the Committee on Analysis of Pre-election Polls and Forecasts*. New York: Social Science Research Council, 1949.

Myrdal, Gunnar. *An American Dilemma: The Negro Problem and Modern Democracy*. New York: Harper and Row, 1962.

Newfield, Jack and Greenfield, Jeff. *A Populist Manifesto: The Making of a New Majority*. New York: Warner, 1972.

Nie, Norman H.; Bent, Dale H.; and Hull, C. Hadlai, *SPSS: Statistical Package for the Social Sciences*. New York: McGraw Hill, 1970.

The 1974 Elections. Congressional Quarterly, Supplement to *Congressional Quarterly Weekly Report* 32, February 23, 1974.

Parkin, Frank. *Class Inequality and Political Order: Social Stratification in Capitalist and Communist Societies*. New York: Praeger, 1971.

Petersen, Svend. *A Statistical History of the American Presidential Elections*. New York: Frederick Ungar, 1968.

Piven, Frances Fox and Cloward, Richard A. *Regulating the Poor: The Functions of Public Welfare*. New York: Vintage Books, 1971.

Politics in America: Edition IV. Washington, D.C.: Congressional Quarterly, 1971.

Rintala, Marvin. "Political Generations." in *International Encyclopedia of the Social Sciences*. New York: Macmillan, 1968. Vol. 6.

Rusk, Jerrold G. and Weisberg, Herbert F. "Perceptions of Presidential Candidates: Implications for Electoral Change." *Midwest Journal of Political Science* 16, 1972, pp. 388-410.

Ryder, Norman B. "The Cohort as a Concept in the Study of Social Change." *American Sociological Review* 30, 1965, pp. 843-61.

Scammon, Richard M. and Wattenberg, Ben J. *The Real Majority*. New York: Coward, McCann, and Georghegan, 1971.

Schattschneider, E.E. *The Semisovereign People: A Realist's View of Democracy in America*. New York: Holt, Rinehart and Winston, 1960.

Searing, Donald D.; Schwartz, Joel J.; and Lind, Alden E. "The Structuring Principle: Political Socialization and Belief Systems." *American Political Science Review* 67, 1973, pp. 415-32.

Sears, David O. "Political Socialization," in Fred I. Greenstein and Nelson W. Polsby, eds. *Handbook of Political Science. Volume 2: Theoretical Aspects of Micropolitics*. Reading, Massachusetts: Addison-Wesley, 1975, in press.

Shively, W. Phillips. "Party Identification, Party Choice, and Voting Stability: The Weimar Case," *American Political Science Review* 66, 1972, pp. 1203-25.

Simon, Julian L. *Basic Research Methods in Social Science: The Art of Empirical Investigation*. New York: Random House, 1969.

Stone, Chuck. *Black Political Power in America*. Indianapolis: Bobbs-Merrill, 1968.

Sundquist, James L. *Dynamics of the Party System: Alignment and Realignment of Political Parties in the United States.* Washington, D.C.: The Brookings Institution, 1973.

de Tocqueville, Alexis. *De la Démocratie en Amérique*. Paris: Union Générale d'Éditions, 1963.

———. *Democracy in America*. Phillips Bradley, ed. New York: Vintage Books, 1945.

U.S. Bureau of the Census, *1970 Census of the Population: General Social and Economic Characteristics*. Washington, D.C.: U.S. Government Printing Office, 1972.

———. *Historical Statistics of the United States: Colonial Times to the Present*. Washington, D.C.: U.S. Government Printing Office, 1972.

———. *Statistical Abstract of the United States: 1972*, 93d edition. Washington, D.C.: U.S. Government Printing Office, 1972.

U.S. Department of Labor, *Manpower Report of the President*. Washington, D.C.: U.S. Government Printing Office, 1973.

Index

Index

Abortion reform, 99
Abramson, Paul R., 41n, 44n
Adams, John Quincy, 1
Age-group differences: among blacks, 65-68, 83, 95; among the middle class, 42-45; in attitudes toward issues, 44-45, 77-83, 104-105, 109-112, 119-120; in class voting, 30-35, 38n, 39-41, 46; in feelings toward groups, 88-96, 104, 106-110, 113-120; in levels of party identification, 53, 55-65; in social composition of Democratic presidential coalition, 46-48; in status polarization, 29-30, 34, 36, 39-41. *See also* Cohort analysis
Agricultural Readjustment Act, 9
Agricultural sector, 2-3, 6, 9, 12-13
Alford, Robert R., 7-8, 13-14, 30
The American Voter. See Campbell, Angus, et al.
Amnesty, 99
Apoliticals, 65-67
Apter, David E., 71-74
Attitudes toward issues: age-group differences in, 44-45, 77-83, 104-105, 109-112, 119-120; among blacks, 76-77, 83; among the middle class, 44-45; by educational level, 77-83; and party identification, 109-112, 119-120; and presidential vote, 44-45, 100-102, 104-105, 109. *See also* Government activism index; Spatial questions
Axelrod, Robert, 23n

Bell, Daniel, 12
Bent, Dale H., 84n
Berelson, Bernard R., 21
Black militants, feelings toward. *See* Feelings toward groups
Blacks: age-group differences among, 65-68, 83, 95; attitudes toward issues, 76-77, 83; class voting of, 9, 20; coalitions with, 25, 71-74, 83, 95, 120, 124; contribution to Democratic presidential coalition, 8-9, 23-26, 46-47; Democratic appeals to, 9, 21, 25-26, 99; and electoral system, 25n; feelings toward groups, 86-95; Goldwater and, 20, 65; migration from South, 13; Nixon and, 20, 22, 99; party identification of, 65-68; political participation of, 3-4, 6, 7n, 8-9, 23-24, 65n, 67n, 71, 123; racial voting, 9, 22; Republicanism among, 9, 65-68; urbanization of, 13; white attitudes toward, 25, 44n, 72. *See also* Attitudes toward issues; Feelings toward groups
Bourgeois radicals, 71-72, 76
Breckinridge, John C., 2
Britain, 11
Brown, Thad A., 86n
Bryan, William Jennings, 3
Bunch, Ralph, 9
Burnham, Walter Dean, 3, 4n, 72-73
Burr, Aaron, 1
Busing, 76, 99, 125

Calhoun, John C., 1
Campbell, Angus, et al., 13-14, 29-30, 34, 37, 51-56, 63, 67n, 68, 123, 125
Campus protestors, 99
Campus unrest, attitudes toward. *See* Attitudes toward issues
Canada, 11
Catholics. *See* Religion
Center for Political Studies of the University of Michigan, 67n, 100. *See also* Survey Research Center
Chicanos, 21
CIO, 6
Civil Rights Act of 1964, 65
Civil rights leaders, feelings toward. *See* Feelings toward groups
Class-based partisanship: changes in, 51-52; defined, 52n
Class voting: age-group differences in, 30, 34-35, 38n, 39-41, 46; among blacks, 9, 20; defined, 7, 8n, 14n, 17n; in postwar elections, 19-20, 41; in prewar elections, 7-8, 20
Clay, Henry, 1
Cohort analysis: defined, 30n; limitations of, 125; methodological problems with, 30n, 39, 56n, 60n, 61n, 62n, 64n, 65n, 78n

137

Congress, 1-2, 6, 25n, 60
Congressional caucus, 1
Converse, Philip E., 3, 63, 67n. *See also* Campbell, Angus, et al.
Coolidge, Calvin, 4
Counterculture, attitudes toward, 84, 86, 99-100, 119. *See also* Feelings toward groups
Cox, James M., 4
Crawford, William H., 1

Davis, John W., 4
Democratic party: attitudes toward issues and, 44-45, 100-101, 104-105, 109-112, 119-120; black support for, 8-9, 22, 25-26, 65-67; feelings toward groups and, 100, 102-104, 106-110, 113-120; history of, 1-4, 6-9; identification with, 53-54; middle-class support for, 6-8, 19, 22-23, 40, 42-45; nominating convention of 1972, 99; party rules, 26, 99, 109, 120-121; social composition of presidential coalition, 9, 23-26, 46-48; working-class support for, 7-8, 19-23
Democratic-Republicans, 1
Depression, 4, 13, 29-30
"Depression generation," 29-30, 34, 37, 38n
Douglas, Stephen A., 2
Duncan, Otis Dudley, 29, 124

Eagleton, Thomas F., 99
Educational level: measurement problems, 78n; presidential voting and, 41n; validity of, 73-74. *See also* Attitudes toward issues; Feelings toward groups
Eisenhower, Dwight D., 20, 38, 42, 45, 61
Electoral College, 1-2
Electoral system, 25n
Ethnic origins, 2, 43

Factor analysis, 84-86
Fair Deal, 21
Fair Employment Practices Commission, 21
Federalists, 1
Feelings toward groups: age-group differences in, 88-96, 104, 106-110, 113-120; among blacks, 86-88, 95; by educational level, 88-96; and party identification, 109-110, 113-120; and presidential vote, 100, 102-104, 106-109. *See also* Feeling thermometer
Feeling thermometer: described, 84-85; measurement problems, 86n, 88n
Fifteenth Amendment, 3, 9
Florida primary, 99
Fortune poll, 9
Functionally superfluous, 71-73, 76

Gallup data: problems with, 20n, 21n, 62-63; results of, 7-8, 20, 40n, 41n, 62-65, 67n
Generational change, 41-42, 45-48, 63-65, 67, 69, 123-125
Generational explanation, 29, 37-40, 53, 55, 60-61, 68, 83, 96, 123-125
Generations, conflicts between, 78, 83, 88, 95-96
Glenn, Norval D., 7-8, 20, 21n, 39, 40n, 41n, 61n, 62-64
Goldwater, Barry M., 20-21, 65, 99n, 100
Government activism index, 44
Government job guarantees, support for, 44-45
Greenfield, Jeff, 25
Guttman scales, 76

Hamilton, Richard F., 19, 21-22
Harding, Warren G., 4
Hefner, Ted, 62-63
Hoover, Herbert C., 4, 9
Hull, C. Hadlai, 84n
Humphrey, Hubert H., 25, 42, 46n
Hyman, Herbert H., 29

Independents. *See* Party identification

Jackson, Andrew, 1-2
Jefferson, Thomas, 1
Jennings, M. Kent, 63-65
Johnson, Lyndon B., 20-22, 25, 42

Kennedy, John F., 21, 25, 42
Kennedy, Robert F., 25
Key, V.O., Jr., 51
Korpi, Walter, 14

Landon, Alfred M., 7
Law and order, 99
Leuchtenburg, William E., 6
Levitin, Teresa E., 86n
Life-cycle explanation, 29, 37-40, 55-56, 60, 67-68, 83, 96, 123-125
Literary Digest polls, 6-7
Lubell, Samuel, 21n

McGovern, George, 19, 23, 25, 41-43, 45-46, 73, 83, 99-100, 104, 109
Marijuana users, feelings toward. *See* Feelings toward groups
Matthews, Donald R., 65n
Middle class. *See* Social class
Middle stratum, 71-73, 124
Military, feelings toward, 99. *See also* Feelings toward groups
Miller, Arthur H., 86n, 99n
Miller, Warren E., 63, 86n. *See also* Campbell, Angus, et al.
Ministers who lead protest marches, feelings toward. *See* Feelings toward groups
Minority groups, attitudes toward. *See* Attitudes toward issues
Monroe, James, 1
Myrdal, Gunnar, 9

National Labor Relations Act, 6
National Opinion Research Center (NORC), 7n, 8-9, 23n
National Recovery Act, 9
Negroes, feelings toward. *See* Feelings toward groups
New Deal, 6-7, 11, 21, 73
Newfield, Jack, 25
New York (state), 120
Nie, Norman H., 84n
Niemi, Richard G., 63-65
Nineteenth Amendment, 4n
Nixon, Richard M., 19-20, 22, 40, 41n, 99-100, 109
Nominating conventions, 1-2, 26, 99-100
"Normalcy," 4

Party identification: age-group differences in 53, 56-65, 67-68; attitudes toward issues and, 109-112, 119-120; among blacks, 65-68; decline of, 52-53, 56-65; defined, 51; father's party, 43-45; feelings toward groups and, 109-110, 113-120; social class and, 19, 51-52
Policemen, feelings toward. *See* Feelings toward groups
Political attitudes. *See* Attitudes toward issues; Feelings toward groups
Political participation, 4-6, 8-9, 14, 25, 46, 65n, 67n
Populists, 2-4
Post-industrial society, 12
Professionals, 19, 40-41, 73
Protestants. *See* Religion
Prothro, James W., 65n

Quotas, 26, 99

Race. *See* Blacks
Radical students, feelings toward. *See* Feelings toward groups
Raine, Alden S., 86n
Regional differences, 1-6, 7n, 8n, 9, 12-13, 19n, 20n, 39, 65n, 67n
Religion, 2-4, 6, 21, 40n, 43-45
Republican party: black support for, 8, 65-68; candidate appeals, 60; history of, 2-4, 7-9; nominating convention of 1972, 100; working-class support for, 40n, 41n, 42
Right-to-work laws, 12
Rintala, Marvin, 37
Roosevelt, Franklin D., 4, 6, 7-9, 67
Roosevelt, Theodore, 4
Rusk, Jerrold G., 76

Scammon, Richard M., 25
Schattschneider, E.E., 3
Schmitz, John, 19n
Sex differences, 4n, 12, 62n, 73
Smith, Alfred E., 6
Social class: change in class structure, 12; and Democratic presidential coalition, 23-26, 46-48; manual-nonmanual dichotomy, 19; middle-class voting, 7-8, 19-20, 22-23, 40, 42-45; and party identification, 19, 51-52; and postwar presidential voting, 13-14, 15-17, 19-23, 29-35, 39-42; and pre-Depression politics, 2-3; and prewar presidential voting, 6-8, 20; service workers, 7, 12; and support

Social class (cont.)
    for Roosevelt, 6-8; working-class voting, 7-8; 19-20; 22-23, 40. *See also* Class voting; Status polarization
South. *See* Regional differences
Spatial questions, 44, 74-76
SPSS (Statistical Package for the Social Sciences), 84
Status polarization: age-group differences in, 29-30, 34, 36, 39-41; defined, 14, 18n; in postwar elections, 13-14, 18-19, 29-30, 34, 36, 41; problems with, 14
Stevenson, Adlai E., 21
Stokes, Donald E., 63. *See also* Campbell, Angus, et al.
Sundquist, James L., 3
Survey Research Center of the University of Michigan (SRC), 12, 14, 19-20, 21n, 39, 43n, 51, 53n, 61, 73-76, 84, 86n, 99

Taft-Hartley Act, 21
Taft, William Howard, 4
Technologically competent, 71-73, 86, 96
Technologically obsolescent, 71-73, 86. *See also* Middle stratum
Television, effects of, 60, 68

de Tocqueville, Alexis, 2-3
Truman, Harry S., 21, 25
Twelfth Amendment, 1

Unions, 2, 6, 11-12
Universities, attitudes toward, 72. *See also* Attitudes toward issues; Feelings toward groups
Urban rioters, feelings toward. *See* Feelings toward groups
Urban unrest, attitudes toward. *See* Attitudes toward issues

Vietnam War, 74, 76, 99

Wallace, George C., 19-20, 22, 25-26, 40-41, 42n, 99
Watergate, 67
Wattenberg, Ben J., 25
Weighting procedures, 21n, 60n, 62n
Weisberg, Herbert F., 76
Whigs, 2
Whites, feelings toward. *See* Feelings toward groups
Wilson, Woodrow, 4
Women's liberation movement, 99. *See also* Feelings toward groups
Working class. *See* Social class

About the Author

Paul R. Abramson is associate professor of political science at Michigan State University. He has contributed articles to numerous journals, including the *American Political Science Review, Comparative Politics, Comparative Political Studies, Journal of Politics, Political Studies*, and the *Public Opinion Quarterly*. Much of the research for this book was conducted while Dr. Abramson was a Ford Foundation Faculty Research Fellow.

DATE DUE

30 505 JOSTEN'S

MONTGOMERY COLLEGE LIBRARIES
germ, circ Generational JK 271.A27

0 0000 00148018 5